THE
PURPOSE

MICHAEL HALL

PAGE PUBLISHING, INC.
New York, NY

First originally published by Page Publishing, Inc. 2019

ISBN 978-1-68456-862-8 (Paperback)
ISBN 978-1-68456-863-5 (Digital)

Printed in the United States of America

ACKNOWLEDGMENT

It has taken forty-six years to finally put down on paper an incident which occurred during the Vietnam War by "friendly fire." Surely I believe there were many more untold incidents, but this personal monster was imbedded, not only in me, but also in other vets. Wounds are not always visible; feelings of guilt, shame, worthlessness, and failure were further fueled by the spit from our own country. We were abandoned by our government, who put us in Vietnam, in harm's way; and upon returning, we had to prove it.

To try to express the actual feelings of losing a game is much easier than expressing loss associated with war. You can blame the coach, the weather, or the other team, and the majority of people would understand and use their judgment to pick a side. Now try to imagine Vietnam like a game. The objective was to win. We had more than enough of everything to win; the commander-in-chief— the president—the best generals, the Congress and Senate, and the American people. Or did we?

That monster started to grow. The feeling of not belonging to this great team was unreal. Were we now the bad guys? We feared not our enemy any longer, but our own. The term "going back to the world," the round eyes were replaced for home and friends. The monster was now completely engorged. We were baby killers and needed to be exterminated.

No more of everything, no more leadership, no more plans to win, the commander-in-chief, Congress, and Senate threw in the towel and, more or less, stated, "You're on your own." *Retreat* is just a word to most people. *Fall back, abandon the firebase, abort the mission* is a wound; death is more becoming than to accept a soldier facing

3

the round eyes back in the world. The constant echoes in our heads, stirred by that monster, now having its way, "Sorry we don't accept your membership to the Veteran of Foreign War Post due to being losers. We won ours!" "Sorry you don't qualify!" "Agent Orange, you sure? You don't qualify."

Putting this incident down on paper is my therapy in coping with the round eyes and to encourage those many vets that are carrying this monster to heal themselves. I've told myself "everything happens for a reason," and it took all these years to have it finally validated in the magazine *Veterans of Foreign Wars*.

How did I end up in this situation? I was sitting on a bar stool, looking into the mirror behind the bar at my own reflection. I was just across the street at the American Legion for veterans, listening to all the heroic stories on how many tours were served in the war. I only needed one tour to know that was all I needed. The only reason I stopped at the American Legion was the gun, a Howitzer, displayed outside the building. That was my gun in the war and the same type of Howitzer I was in charge of, Gun 6.

As I listened and watched everyone at the American Legion, a strange feeling of guilt and worthlessness was amidst. I knew that feeling—a curse, present and devouring everyone. With each drink they took, their stories would always change, and this was how I ended up on this bar stool staring at my reflection. I just needed to clear my head, and I knew I'd catch hell later at home. Home was another war, along with my disability war with the government, and now the war with the Veteran's Hospital.

The Veteran's Hospital informed me that I have no spinal fluid around my spinal cord. There was a severe narrowing of the spinal canal with indentation of the ventral cord at cervical level 3-4; I learned medical terms. I also had a ruptured tendon of the bicep muscle on my right arm that could not be repaired. Funny, that was years ago, and I was still waiting for that MRI report for their plan of treatment—promised but never delivered. I asked for a meeting with the director of the Veteran's Hospital, but it also never came. I quit going to the Veteran's Hospital. My primary doctor wrote a memo a year later to the chief of neurosurgery to remind him of the unfinished report, but a response also never came, so I self-medicated my pain with the company of gentlemen from Kentucky. They lived in a bottle and provided a quick attitude adjustment.

"Those real?" the fella sitting next to me was asking, pointing at my dog tags, which had slipped out of my shirt.

"They're as real as the monsoon floods they went through, blown and whipped around from the winds, dragged through mud from the top of mountain firebases, and splattered by blood, sweat, and tears. Yes, sir, they're real!"

"Not to change the subject," I asked, "but are you real?"

"What do you mean, am I real?" he responded.

"I'm sorry to ask, but you have a strong resemblance to Leonardo DiCaprio, the actor," I stated.

"I get that a lot. Here, look at my pictures on my cell phone. I run into a lot of famous people. Look at their autographs. Actually, it's my sister who knows these people. When I go to her house, you never know who is visiting. Her husband is a very successful agent, from sports to movies!" he remarked.

"The only thing I have as an autograph is an old letter addressed to me from the president," I said.

"Yeah, right." He laughed.

"You want to see it?" I asked.

"You have it?" He was surprised.

"I was going to throw it in the trash. I'll go get it from my car."

I opened my album to the letter so he could read it and slipped off to the little boy's room. When I returned, the expression on his face had changed, and his questions were endless. He wanted to know what happened. And when I finished the account of the incident, he was speechless. I said I had to go, but he grabbed my arm remarking, "This, you have to write down, everything that happened from the beginning and the truth. You have to tell the truth. You should come back here, and I'll buy you a beer, okay?" he said. "What's your name?" he asked.

As I walked out of the bar, I turned around and said, "Michael Angelo."

I kept hearing the words "the truth" over and over in my head. As a child, was I taught the *truth*. Looking back, how was I associated with the truth? I believed I was taught right and wrong. As a child, and once I learned the language, it was right to pretend to be a cowboy and wrong to be an Indian. Was it right to allow terrorists from another county to invade, take and kill the name of justice and democracy? Was it right for the president, back then Andrew Jackson, to offer every person twenty dollars for every Indian scalp, whether man, woman, or child? Was it right to use another human's blood and sweat for your own benefit? Was it wrong to be a man of color?

My three daughters had all seen and lived hardship in their youths. I apologize every day for not being able to give them more, but they understood how my life was as a boy, secluded from the outside world. And as their father, they saw and lived every failure I attempted. One day, my daughter, Michele, came to me and asked mysteriously, "Dad, did you sell your soul to the devil? Nothing ever goes right for you, and we know you try so hard."

Thinking back now that they're all grown, I have ten grandchildren and two great-grandchildren. I've always told them that you can only control the things you can control in your own life. I've taught them to be good people. If you see someone that's hungry, feed them. If you see someone thirsty, give them drink. If you see someone hurt, help them, cry with them. And if someone gets a good break, laugh and celebrate with them. These actions you can control.

"Thank you, Devin Michael," I said.

"For what, PaPa?" he asked.

"For helping send the letter to my daughter," I remarked.

"PaPa, you're my PaPa, I'll do anything for you," he remarked. "Remember when you told me that you always have my back and take care of me?" he asked. "Well, PaPa, I got your back. Nothing or no one will sneak up on you. You're my only PaPa, and I'll take care of you just like you have been taking care of me for fourteen years, from the time I was born. I too, PaPa, never had a father. You've given me everything I wanted and never flinched when I asked for it.

I know you love me with all your heart, and that's ditto for me too!" he stated.

"But why did you throw your war album away? I found it in the trash. It's all you have to remember. Not everyone gets a letter from the president of the United States like you did," he stated. "And how about the award the United States Army gave you? It was given to you, PaPa, and states to Specialist Four, Michael Angelo. What's that all about, Papa?" he asked.

"That was my rank when I came back from Vietnam. I finished my service in Fort Knox, Kentucky," I answered.

"But, Papa," he stated. "In the war you said you were a Sergeant E-5, a section chief of Gun 6?" he questioned.

"They never promoted me to Sergeant E-5 when I came home. I was demoted to E-4," I answered.

"That wasn't right, Papa, and they did you wrong. Plus you never received your war metals for serving," he remarked. "So this award from the United States Army was when you came back to the States as the number 1 man on the number 3 piece? What's that?" he questioned.

"Remember, when I was in the war, I became the number 1 man on gun section number 1. I was the fastest loader on the firebase. No one could load faster! At Fort Knox, Kentucky, I was placed in a mobile unit, self-propelled 155 Tank Artillery Howitzer, and I became the loader and number 1 man. Our unit was being tested for technical proficiency inspection and operational readiness. I informed our section chief that I could outload and finish the fire mission faster than any of the other gun sections, and he stated, 'Go for it!'"

"Well, you must have done it because it states on your award 'Your professional expertise, devotion to duty and exemplary performance contributed immeasurably to the extremely high rating received by his unit during the test period and reflects great credit upon himself and the United States Army.' How cool was that, Papa? You were a bad dude, really," he boasted.

"Son, when I came back, I was a shell of a man and full of shame. I was spit on, booed, and yelled at with things thrown at me.

We were called baby killers, murderers, and it brought tears to my eyes knowing how much our country hated us. I took my gun section inside the airport restaurant for our first steak dinner with fries and a cold beer. When dinner was served, people had spit in the food and beer. We got up and went to the lobby and waited until each flight departed. We never saw each other again. We all had gone in different directions home.

"Son, there's times when you don't want to remember incidents which occurred in your life, right or wrong, you can't control it. That's when I fall into my own world and remember the good times, like when you were born," I said.

"Papa, I need you, and will always need you in my life. Tell me when it all started, just think back...," he asked.

In a small Indian fishing village, a baby's cry could be heard. It came from a wooden shack with a dirt floor, and there was nothing in the room but blankets on the dirt floor to lie on. There was a young woman, a mother, whose face showed both joy and sadness at the same time. There was no doctor for delivery and no birth certificate stating time of birth. It was just another day and a new baby born.

"What's his name?" someone asked.

The mother looked at her newborn son and remarked, "His name is Miguel Angel."

This was the beginning of life for Michael Angelo. As his second day of life started, his brothers and sisters, who were much older, came to see him. Michael Angelo was number 10 to his new family, but only nine had survived. A brother, who was a year older, had passed away due to a blood infection. Another sister was not present as she was given up to an orphanage due to the lack of food for the family. The people in the village expressed disgust rather than joy toward a mother whose path of survival for her family led to begging, stealing, and using her body to feed her family. She had no one to help her, no husband or father to any of her children. Day after day, night after night, she locked all nine children in the shack so no one would hurt them, while she walked all night to find what little food she could for them. The nights were filled with fear as shadows from the outside reflected through the slats of their broken-down home.

But the sound of the lock being opened in the morning by a tired, weary face took away all those fears for the chance to eat a small bag of beans or rice.

As time turned into days, and days turned into months, and months turned into years, the burden of watching the little one was having an impact on the older brothers and sisters. They themselves wanted to search for food. It was easier to slip away to the fishing pier, where the chances of catching a fish were better than watching Michael Angelo. But Michael Angelo knew their plan, so he pretended to be asleep, and when they snuck away at night, Michael Angelo would follow them, keeping out of sight, until he was too far from home, and they could not take him home. Oh boy, were they angry when they spotted him following behind, but they were not going back. So they took Michael Angelo with them to the fishing pier, and once there, they told him to stay in the middle of the pier so they would not have to worry about him falling off into the water.

As Michael Angelo watched his brothers and sisters fishing for hours with no luck in catching anything, Michael Angelo sat on the pier and saw a hole. He looked through the hole in the pier and saw there were big fish right below him. With excitement, and quietness, Michael Angelo collected pieces of fishing lines, tying them together. And as luck would have it, he found a hook. Scraping up a piece of dry fish on the pier, he lowered the hook down into the water. No sooner did the bait hit the water, bam, and fish on. Michael Angelo screamed with excitement, holding onto the fishing line as it was jerking violently. It took all the strength he had. Hearing Michael Angelo's screams, his brother grabbed the fishing line and started to bring the fish up. He then realized the hole was too small, which made everyone angry.

"You told me to stay in the middle," Michael Angelo responded. No one spoke to Michael Angelo for the rest of the day.

The following day, the mother heard that a crab boat was coming in with a large load of crabs, and when the people in the village heard the sound of the factory whistle, they came running with any type of bucket. The whistle sounded, and people ran to the boat docks as fast as they could. Michael Angelo looked like a flag flapping in the wind as he was grabbed by his sibling. The walk back was much slower as everyone was enjoying the sweet taste of the crab legs, and their buckets were full of crabs, which made everyone very happy.

Days and months continued, but surviving was not getting any easier. At times, Michael Angelo's only nourishment was nursing on his mother's breast for food until the day she howled, "You're killing me, Michael Angelo, and I can't do it anymore." On that day, Michael Angelo started sucking dirt for food. Everything that his brothers and sisters could do for food, they did.

Playing outside in the dirt with some other children, Michael Angelo spotted a three-legged chair. While trying to balance on it, the chair collapsed, and Michael Angelo did not see the rusty nail protruding under the seat of the chair, which jetted through his upper lip, ripping his lip wide open. It was chaos among his mother, brothers and sisters, and other people nearby, as they tried to stop the bleeding. With every scream from Michael Angelo, blood would fill his mouth, causing him to choke, spit, and cough. Until someone mixed some cement together with water and packed his lip with it. It stopped the bleeding, to everyone's amazement. The healing process seemed like it took forever, because there was no doctor or medicine available. With his lip sticking out, swollen and sensitive, sucking at his mother's breast was out of the question.

One day, everyone went on a hunting trip in an open field. One of Michael Angelo's older brothers became an expert with a slingshot, which he made. He spotted a sparrow, aimed, and shot. He started a fire, and the family sat around it, watching as he cooked the bird. It was the best-tasting bird. To Michael Angelo, it was the size of a turkey.

The time had come when Michael Angelo was used in a scheme to relieve the fruit man of his goods. The fruit man would push his beautiful cart of oranges up and down the street to sell. The sight and smell of those huge oranges was too much to pass up. Michael Angelo was the smallest and quickest, as his siblings would find out, when they tried to sneak away to keep from watching him.

Michael Angelo's clothes were always too large; his pants would drag, and his T-shirt was like a dress on him, which, in the scheme of the plan, would work excellent. So the plan was drawn out, making sure Michael Angelo understood his part, and he was told he would be the hero of it all. The first part of the plan was for the older ones to beg for pennies from anyone who would give them one. At the end of the day, they would, if lucky, have five to six pennies. The second part of the plan was to watch when the fruit man would stop by several shacks, where maybe two or three people would come out to buy some oranges. The third part of plan was to wait until the fruit man would present his oranges, so beautiful and shiny, stacked like a pyramid, so everyone could see how many he had. The fourth part of the plan was for the older children to walk to the fruit cart like everyone else, knowing the fruit man would be keeping a sharp eye on them. The fifth part of the plan was to make sure Michael Angelo was placed between the shacks and the cart so he could see everything happening.

Now they all made a circle to show how the plan would work. The older ones would walk to the fruit cart and stand near the fruit man so he could hear the jingling of pennies, making it sound like they had lots of money to spend. One of them would remark how beautiful the oranges looked for distraction, and other siblings would walk around the cart to select the oranges they wanted. Someone would pull an orange from the bottom of the pyramid, causing all the oranges to fall onto the street. Everyone would make it look like they were helping the fruit man collect his oranges while kicking some of the oranges farther away or beneath the cart, and all the while, Michael Angelo was collecting as many as he could carry in his overly large T-shirt. Everyone would then run back and forth between the shacks and wait until all the commotion had settled as the fruit man retrieved his oranges that had fallen to the ground. Mother never could understand how all these oranges appeared, nor did everyone else. It was puzzling, but they sure were good and sweet.

This plan would work for only several more times. Always, the fruit man remarked how clumsy these kids were and never seeing Michael Angelo under his fruit cart. Then one day, when they all came home, with no luck in every scheme, they found oranges, candy, food, clothes, and their mother had money and toy cars, dolls, and kites. Who did Mother rob, they thought? It took Mother several minutes to collect herself, while they checked out all the gifts that someone had left. Was this a dream, and if it was, don't let it stop!

Finally, Mother spoke, "An American couple came and gave me all these gifts. They wanted to know how many children I had, and who was the youngest."

That was when everyone looked at Michael Angelo and wondered, what were Americans and where did they come from? Then the thought hit them, they must have seen Michael Angelo under the fruit cart taking all those oranges, and now they were here to take him to jail, and leaving all these gifts for taking him away. Mother did not go out that night in search of food. They all knew something was about to happen, but what?

Early the next morning, the whole village was gathering around a big black bus; it looked like a bug, but someone said it was called a car. The American couple had come back with more food, fruit, candy, toys, and money. They had never seen a white person before and were amazed but at the same time scared; and they talked differently too. They opened the door to this big black bug, and everyone gasped. Out stepped the "Missing One." Mother screamed and started to cry out loud. So did all the older siblings, but Michael Angelo did not know why. This was his sister, the Missing One, which he never knew. His sister ran into her mother's arms crying, and together the whole family was hugging and crying, except for Michael Angelo, who stood outside the circle of weeping bodies. He watched everyone, crying and hugging, but did not understand what was happening and became scared, backing up and wanting to run.

Michael Angelo had never seen a car, so when he saw this huge object, which, in his mind, looked like a big black bug, it scared him. Americans got out of this big black bug, but he had never seen a white person before, and this also scared the poop out of him. Americans talked so differently, and they had a woman with them who talked like Michael Angelo and then talked like them. Michael Angelo became really scared when they stopped talking and turned to look and point at him. Michael Angelo didn't know, but that was going to be the last time he would see his mother and most of his brothers and sisters again.

The American couple had found the Missing One, his sister, in an orphanage during their search to adopt a child. When they found the Missing One, they asked her if she had a brother. Arrangements were made, and legal papers drawn up. Mother knew she could not feed and raise the two youngest children but wanted a better life from them. Her heart broke, as did the hearts of siblings, when a young mother moved toward Michael Angelo, who was crying in fear. She knelt down beside him and comforted him, telling him that she could no longer feed him or the Missing One. She could no longer care of them. "These people, Americans, were not here to hurt you. Just the opposite, they are here to give you both food, clothes, toys, and a beautiful warm house with your own room."

Michael Angelo looked at the Missing One and said, "I don't know the Missing One. I don't even know her name. Can you come with us, Mother?"

"Michael Angelo," she said, "I cannot go with you and your sister. I still have the others to take care of. You both are the youngest."

Michael Angelo asked his mother, "Can you come visit us where we are going?"

"Michael Angelo," she spoke softly. "This place is far, far away and so much prettier than this place. Michael Angelo, you have to be brave and strong. These people are not going to hurt you. I promise you." She hugged Michael Angelo's trembling body as he started to cry. "Now," she said, "it's time to go."

It took all the strength of the white people to get Michael Angelo and his sister, the Missing One, into that big black bug. Screaming and crying, the Missing One grabbed their mother's arm through the window, biting it, as the car pulled away.

The drive was long with all the crying and screaming, exhausting both Michael Angelo and the Missing One. They soon fell asleep. Both were awakened by the sounds of many people walking, talking everywhere, and many cars honking their horns. The smell of food was wafting through the air. Had they arrived in the place that was far, far away, they wondered? Michael Angelo listened to the people talking, and some of them spoke the same language. Where were they?

The woman that spoke two languages said, "It's getting to be nighttime, and your parents are getting a room at the hotel."

The Missing One spoke, "Did you say parents?"

The woman remarked, "Yes, these people are your new father and mother, you are their children."

Before the Missing One could ask another question, the new people came back and motioned them to a door that opened by itself, which scared them both. Once inside the door, it closed by itself again, which further scared them. They hugged each other in fear. The woman pushed a button, and all of a sudden, the floor fell down, causing them both to scream. The woman said, "Oops, I pushed the wrong button."

All of a sudden, the floor stopped, and the door opened. Right in front of them was a blazing fire from a huge furnace. A man with his back turned away from the door suddenly turned around. Michael Angelo and the Missing One screamed, "El Diablo, El Diablo!" The man was black in color, as though he had been burned. They both crammed against the back of the little moving room screaming, "El Diablo, El Diablo!"

The woman pushed the button again, and the floor went up, up, up. Michael Angelo and the Missing One dropped to their knees, shaking with fear. The woman calmed them down saying, "No, no that's not the devil, it's just a black man, a Negro man."

That night, Michael Angelo and the Missing One received their first bath in a bathtub filled with warm water, water that came out of handles. They slept in beds that were soft and warm and clothes, called pajamas, with slippers that were soft and warm. They were given cookies and warm milk to make them happy.

The following morning, Michael Angelo and his sister—he still didn't know her name—were taken to be fitted with new clothes and shoes. They walked around from store to store. His sister noticed some people had slanted eyes, some people were black, and some people were white. All the people looked and spoke different.

The woman who spoke "two voices" told both children that Michael Angelo was going to get his first haircut so that he can get his picture taken. When they were done, they were taken to the doctor's office where they were checked out medically and given shots so that they could cross the border into the Unites States of America. As Michael Angelo's sister was taken into the doctor's office to get her shots, Michael Angelo waited his turn outside. When she came out with tears in her eyes, he was taken in. When Michael Angelo was in the exam room, his sister came running in and grabbed Michael Angelo's arm just as the doctor was giving the shot with an air gun, causing him to get two shots instead of one. They both ran out of the office crying and screaming. The man and woman comforted them both and said it was all over, now they could go to their new home.

Michael Angelo and his sister arrived at their new home, and they had never seen anything so beautiful. A huge house with three bedrooms, a bathroom, a kitchen, another room called a living room with a TV that neither of them understood. There was a yard in front of the house and another area in the back of the house with a swing set. And there was a house to put the big black bug inside called a garage. Michael Angelo and his sister never would have imagined that life could be like this. There was not one pair of pants which was always dirty and didn't fit, but a clean pair of pants and a shirt for every day of the week. There was a bathroom with clean water, a bathtub that you could lie in for as long as you wanted, and it was not a metal tub with cold water used by all the children. There was a toilet that flushed with toilet paper, not an outhouse outside in the cold, with a hole to sit on filled with flies that constantly landed on you and rags for toilet paper that didn't flush. The house had rooms for everyone and beds so soft and comfortable, with a chest of drawers for putting all your socks and underwear away. Most important, there was electricity in every room. This was not a one-room shack with a dirt floor and only blankets to wrap up in so bugs wouldn't get all over you while you tried to sleep. As soon as they sun went down, so did the light until morning.

There was a yard to play in with swings and a slide. A tree to climb and, most surprising, was something called grass. Grass was so soft to walk barefoot over and to roll around on with a smell so sweet. But all these things made Michael Angelo sad because he remembered what everyone back home did not have, and he was very sad.

Life continued on in this beautiful country, everything perfect, until six months passed, and the adoptive father had a massive heart attack and died, leaving a grief-stricken wife all alone. Their plan was for both of them to raise these new children together. Sadness had entered the household. As a widow, and now a single parent, Michael Angelo's adoptive mother had secluded herself and the two children from the outside world except for school. The children were kept inside a fortress made of a huge ten-foot hedge that surrounded the entire property. No one could see in, and neighbors attempted to befriend his adoptive mother, but to no avail as she kept to herself, and that was to be for the next ten years.

Michael Angelo could see the stress and depression in his adoptive mother, which was understandable due to financial strains after the loss of her husband. His military pension and his work pension were all she had to raise these children. Michael Angelo remembered all the times his real mother had nothing but prayers to go on, the many conversations she had on her knees to this person call Dios, or God. Maybe this person, God, Michael Angelo thought, told her to give him and his sister away to these people.

Michael Angelo's adoptive father was a kind, gentle, and hard-working man. Born in Nebraska, he joined the military at a very young age—Navy submarines, a mechanic. He traveled all over the world. There was a story written in the *Post* magazine about a situation during World War II, against the Japanese, on an island in the Dutch East Indies, in the early 1940s. Before Michael Angelo and his sister were adopted, his father and mother had earlier adopted another child. This child was from Seoul, Korea. He lived in the same house, went to schools here, and his American name was George. The adoptive parents never mentioned or talked about their other son. His Korean name was Kim.

After Michael Angelo's adoptive father had passed away, it took a great toll on his adoptive mother. The stress was obvious, and the anger came out and was directed toward him and his sister.

Dinnertime was the most stressful time. Michael Angelo and his sister could not eat the type of food their adoptive mother would cook. The food consisted of boiled carrots, peas, yellow squash, baked fish, liver, or plain hamburger with no taste. This made their mother very angry, always screaming at them to eat. His sister tried to explain the kind of food they had eaten, but no one understood. This was the first time Michael Angelo had his face pushed into a plate of food. Crying "no, no," she would punish them without dinner and send them to bed. Both terrified kids would fall asleep quickly, and the following morning, both children, still afraid from the night before, were told to sit for breakfast. The food again looked strange, poached eggs on toast and orange juice to drink. Michael Angelo just sat there looking at the strange food. Again, the adoptive mother started screaming at them to eat and cutting the poached egg on their toast.

Michael Angelo's stomach was upset, and he felt the need to throw up. He waited for his face to be pushed into the runny egg yolk, and it was. Michael Angelo's sister yelled, "No, no!" And she ran to the room and locked the door. He just sat there crying and looking at the food. He was finally told to go wash his face and was pushed into his room, where he sat in silence.

School had started, and the fear of not understanding what people were saying was terrifying. Not only that, but the teachers were dressed in black-and-white gowns with their heads covered too; they were called nuns. Michael Angelo and his sister were put into a Catholic school, where everyone was dressed alike. Boys wore pants and white shirts, and the girls wore skirts and white shirts. No one spoke their language, and they were made fun of.

Every day, they learned about this person named Jesus, his days as a child through the day he died on the cross. They also learned about his father, God. It was confusing and the same routine in church every day: standing, kneeling, up and down, all the time. After the first year of school, Michael Angelo was told he could not move up to the second grade because he did not know enough English. This made him very sad as all the other kids went on to the second grade. They all made fun of him, and he could not understand why the teachers did not speak his language. What made it even more confusing was that every day in church, they spoke an additional language called Latin.

Coming home from school was filled with daily emotions of fear knowing that the adoptive mother was going to scream at them about something. Every day, they were told to go outside and play, even on weekends, until they were called in for dinner. Always, as the time came closer for dinner, there was the dreaded thought of what he and his sister were going to be forced to eat. Their stomachs were starting to get very upset. They thought of the beans and rice they used to eat. Forcing themselves to eat all these strange foods, or be screamed at, was very stressful. His sister was four years older than him and would scrape some of her food onto his plate, begging him to help her eat it or she would get into trouble. He helped her out and forced it down while she would wrap the rest of the food in a napkin and put it into her pocket until she got to the trash can. But this worked for only so long, and she got caught one day. Boy, did she get into trouble, getting screamed at and spanked. This only drove his sister further apart as the anger was building up every day in both children at home and at school.

Michael Angelo was behind in English, so when it came time for recess, he was kept from going outside and was told to practice his English over and over. This embarrassed him when all the other children saw him and made fun of him. He promised himself that he'd write better and read better than any of these white kids.

Year after year the only contact with kids their own age was at school. No friends were allowed to come over and play, talk, or watch television. TV was only allowed from six to eight at night, followed by bedtime. They were not allowed to go visit a friend, even if they only lived a few houses down the block. The entire property was wrapped in a thick ten-foot hedge that kept anyone from looking in and kept the children from having contact with the outside world. Peeking through the hedge, Michael Angel and his sister would hear children walking by on their way to a public school only four blocks away, and they did not have to wear uniforms. When they asked to go to that school, the answer was just no. Michael Angelo's sister was four years ahead of him in school. When she finished grade school, she was enrolled into an all-girls Catholic high school, which made her very sad because she wanted to have contact in a public high school. The answer was always no.

As Michael Angelo was finishing his last years in grade school, he was talking fluent English and had lost his native language. The stress his adoptive mother was going through in trying to pay for the tuition for his sister's schooling made it difficult for his tuition payments in grade school. An agreement was made with the Catholic school to keep Michael Angelo enrolled, but he would have to pull weeds, cut grass, and rake leaves at the nuns' convent. This was a low time for him. As the years passed, it became evident he was not going to be enrolled in an all-boys Catholic high school. Pressure finally broke, and both children were put into a public high school, where they now were going to be exposed to the real world.

After a week of public school, Michael Angelo's sister was full of information and excitement from all her newly made friends. How different the schools were. She would state with excitement bubbling out of her, "Everyone wears different types of clothes, not uniforms, no marching to each class like soldiers, or having to freeze when the freeze bell sounded, or going to mass every morning." But that was not all. There was a football game every Friday and dances after the game. His sister loved to dance. "And also cheerleading." She laughed. "When you come here, you can play football, basketball, baseball, tennis, swimming, track—anything you want."

The more she mentioned all these things she called sports, Michael Angelo wondered what she was talking about and how he could play when he didn't even know what they were. Michael Angelo would ask his classmates, but they all laughed that he didn't know how to play any of these games. He took it upon himself to look them up in the dictionary, and how he wished he had a father to teach him.

His sister was allowed to attend the games and stay for the dances as long as a friend's parent brought her home and she followed the rules. But that changed one Friday night when the screaming and yelling started. Michael Angelo was woken up when his sister stayed out longer, and she was not brought home by her friend's parent but a boy from school. That night everything changed at home. No longer was his sister allowed to live at home but was told to move out and let that boy take care of her, so she left. Michael Angelo sat in his room with the feeling of being alone shadowing his entire body with fear just as it did that day he left his mother for the last time.

Time continued passing, and Michael Angelo followed the same routes and rules out of fear and the constant threat that the same would happen to him if he didn't comply; he would find himself homeless with nowhere to go. The time had come when he had entered the same public school exposure his sister experienced with excitement and joy. But not for Michael Angelo; he kept to himself and did not make friends for fear of making a mistake. One day, while watching the football team practice drills, he was asked if he would like to try out for the team. He hurried home to ask his adoptive mother for approval to try out, but she said no. When he asked why not, he was told that he did not know the game, was not in shape, and would end up getting hurt.

From that point forward, Michael Angelo ate all his vegetables and started running around the house every day until his legs ached so bad he could not take another step. He would watch and learn the object of the game. As summer was approaching, he told his mother the football team was open for anyone to train and run, and the weight room was available for use. Reluctantly his mother finally agreed as long as he followed the rules.

That summer after finishing his chores at home, Michael Angelo would walk every day to the high school, work out until noon, then walk home to have lunch and finish whatever his mother needed done at home. He would then walk back to the school and continue to work out until it was time to go back home. This continued for the entire summer. When summer had ended, it was time for Michael Angelo to put all his training into action. He mingled with the rest of the players when they were told to group into positions they wanted to try out for. Now the truth would come out. He told his mother that he understood all the positions of the game even though he did not; generally, he knew the object of the game was to get the ball to the other end of the field. What confused Michael Angelo was the guy shouting numbers out loud and the guy getting the ball—better get it right or a wall of big bodies came crashing down on them.

Now that's what caught his eye. *I can do that*, he thought. *I'm not afraid of being hit or hitting someone who's supposed to be hit.* He found his group. As the training continued, he learned his and all the other positions. Michael Angelo was playing both defense and offense and was labeled as being ruthless and just plain mean by his own teammates. They would complain that he hit them too hard, but he responded that his mother hit harder than they did and added, while laughing, how he couldn't wait until the next practice.

Every day the walk home from school took forever because there was no hurry to get there. It wasn't like you could go home and kick up your feet and relax—not there ever since his sister was told to move out. An emptiness and sadness had consumed Michael Angelo. There was nothing to talk about with his adoptive mother. When it came time to eat dinner, it was placed on the dinner table, and his mother would go into the kitchen, which was divided by a wall, so they couldn't see each other. She would sit in the kitchen, smoke cigarettes, and drink her coffee until he had finished eating. The evenings were mostly filled with silence. He wondered where his sister was, a constant thought. While sitting in his room, there was an overwhelming feeling of being alone; his sister no longer lived with him, and he could see his mother's health was not very good from all those cigarettes she smoked.

One day he heard his name being called from the kitchen where his mother sat smoking cigarettes and sipping on coffee. She motioned him to sit down then stated she was informed that Michael Angelo's second oldest brother had been arrested and was being held in jail. The next day they would drive back to the place he was born.

She finished locking the house up, then placed the lunch she had packed for the trip into the car. She double-checked to see if she had the ID papers to get back into the country before they crossed the border. Michael Angelo thought the border seemed familiar. Then he realized this was the place he and his sister had been nine years ago. She told Michael Angelo that he and his sister came eighty miles south from where they were, and it would take a couple hours to get there. She stated that the name of the fishing village was called Ensenada. Now he finally knew where he was born, Baja, California, which meant "below California"; it was a peninsula.

She continued, "Your people started in the United States, that was their home. The Native Americans were at war with the United States, and they lost and were forced to move onto reservations or prison camps. The ones who refused were hunted down and killed. Anyone who brought an Indian scalp belonging to a man, woman, or child was given a twenty-dollar gold coin. The Native Americans who refused to move onto reservations were divided into two groups. One group went north into Canada, and the other group went south into Mexico."

Michael Angelo remembered this from school. "The Native Americans that stayed on the reservations were called the Hang-Around-the-Fort People, and those who refused and left were called the Traditional People. They did not wait for the soldiers to throw a bone out to them."

*****

We traveled the coastal road toward Ensenada, and the Pacific Ocean was endless. The fishing boats below looked two inches long from the road we were driving. I could imagine centuries ago the bloodline that I belonged to being relocated from their home and traveling this same road toward unknown origins, just like I was doing now. I didn't know where I was going; but not her, she drove with no map like she had traveled these roads many times before. As we entered Ensenada, she again was in control of where our destination was. I had lost my language and could not understand a word of what she was trying to communicate with the people in trying to find the jail. When we found the jail, she told me to follow her and to stay close behind. She led the way right through the jail doors, where we came into contact with men in uniforms. Policemen, I thought. They were taken by surprise by this white woman asking questions about a certain person.

When the policemen saw me, they tried to speak to me, but I froze with fear. I moved behind my adoptive mother to hide. She informed them I was the brother of the person she was seeking. They turned for a few minutes, which seemed like hours to me, and then finally led us inside. The doors were made out of metal with a sliding slot in each for people to look through. When the door opened and we walked through, there were sounds of men talking amongst themselves, wondering what was happening. The guards were carrying all types of guns as they escorted us through the living quarters of the prisoners, who were as amazed to see us, as I was them. We stopped in the back corner of the building, where a mattress laid on the floor, and I recognized my brother. Seeing me, he loudly said, "Michael Angelo, Michael Angelo!"

We both hugged, and I could see he was as happy to see me as I was to see him. Trying to hold back tears was useless. He was my strength as a child, my protector, the one who devised any plan to feed the siblings with each opportunity that came his way. Now, here was my brother in jail. I thought to myself he was caught stealing too many oranges. He tried to communicate with me, but I was embarrassed that I couldn't speak to him for I had lost my language; he understood.

My adoptive mother found a prisoner that could speak both languages, so now we could talk. I learned he was involved with the wrong people and was arrested. As she was getting information from my brother as to how long, what were the charges, how much money, etc., I watched the prisoners going about their daily routine. The majority of prisoners were, what looked like, counting pinto beans into groups, for every person got only so many pinto beans for lunch and dinner. Our meeting was cut short by the guards. The prisoner who spoke two languages told us that we came on the wrong day; next week was the day to come. We were whisked away quickly as I waved goodbye, but it was understood we would be back.

We headed back to the border, and darkness had overtaken us, with the Pacific Ocean no longer visible—just blackness. The thought of a brother with no one to help him hung heavy on my mind and heart. Little did I know that this meeting with my brother would be the last time I would see him. He passed away the week he was released from jail and was found in an old shack. He was so close to maybe communicating with me about the family and didn't even get to ask about our mother. I wanted to know if she was still alive, had passed away, or did my mother not want to see me. Now I would never know that answer. These were the things in life that you had no control over. You never know what tomorrow will bring, and it's how you handle today that can make a difference.

I didn't know that in a few years after my brother's death that my adoptive mother would also pass away. All those cigarettes caught up with her. I also didn't know that before those last few years were over, she had befriended a family that had agreed to take me in if something happened to her. She must have known she was sick and didn't want to tell me. I was the only one living in the house when she was admitted into the hospital. I didn't know how to feel. Was she dying or was she going to get better? The family she befriended would pick me up and drive me to the hospital to visit with her. But each time I went, she didn't look any better, and she reached the point of not being able to speak. One day I lay in the living room sleeping on the couch with most of the lights off, and the telephone rang. It was the hospital calling to tell me she had passed away. Now I was truly alone. I just sat in the darkness not knowing what to do, completely lost and alone.

The family that was supposed to take care of me backed out of the agreement with my adoptive mother. I found that out through a lawyer she had hired to draw up the documents. Since that was not going to happen, the lawyer drew up documents for foster care through the court. I was scared. How to get back across the border was the thought that kept crossing my mind. I didn't even know how to talk the language anymore. I didn't know what to do because now I was a citizen of this country. I was put in a foster home so that I could finish school, but I couldn't care less about school. My biggest fear was what was going to happen after school was finished; mentally, I was lost, and physically, I was alone.

I listened to my classmates and their plans for their futures. Those plans always came back to their parents and how their parents were going to send them to college or teach them a trade so they could make a living. I didn't have parents, and I feared I was going to be homeless, a bum with no job.

Going to school every day was becoming very stressful. My mental abilities were flooded out with worry. At football practice, my anger was being taken out on my teammates, who were beaten black and blue by my constant drilling. I would scream at them, "If you can't stop me, how the hell are you going to stop all the other schools." My practice routines were relentless.

If I wasn't running, I would be in the weight room making myself stronger and quicker than anyone in the room, and they all knew it. On the practice field, I was going to hit them hard, and this was my way of venting my anger. As the football season started, and knowing that this was my last year of school, thoughts of what and how I was going to do after school ended only compelled my anger more on the team. We hadn't won a game, and by the way I saw this team, we weren't going to win one either.

I was eventually introduced to the new foster family, and the adjustment was, of course, awkward. They had another foster child and three children of their own. The other foster child was a young man like me that we went to the same school; however, our schedules were different. I hardly saw him until nighttime after I came back from football practice. The younger children would wait until I arrived home to eat dinner. After finishing dinner, we all went outside into the neighborhood. I was taken aback as to why all these neighborhood kids were hanging around the house; some I recognized from school, but I didn't know them. One of them came over and welcomed me to the neighborhood. He told me he lived next door and also informed me that my foster brother had told everyone that a star football player was living in his house, so everyone wanted to meet me, plus everyone was going to the football game to see me play.

As the final seconds ticked off the clock to another loss, the team ran into the locker room and ran out without taking a shower. I guess they saw my disappointment in the way they played. No one said a word, they just left quickly. I was in no hurry to go anywhere.

By the time I reached the neighborhood, just about everyone was in the street; music was playing, and people were everywhere and having a good time. What did I miss? As I approached the house, the neighbors came running, everyone yelling, "Great game!"

"Did you all go to the right school, because we lost?" I asked.

They told me that they didn't come for the game but to watch the new guy on the block, who through his foster brother's testimony, declared that by watching Michael Angelo practice and play, there was no other player who could go against him. I realized this was why the whole neighborhood showed up for the football game, and I also realized they were not disappointed. I lay in my room that night with the lights off so no one would bother me. I could hear the excitement of the three children belonging to the foster family. They kept repeating the whole game, on how many tackles, sacks, and recovered fumbles I made that night. It was like hearing a broken record over and over until their mother sent them to bed. "Michael Angelo lives with us" echoed down the hallway.

The football season ended, and just as I predicted, not a game was won. I was glad it was over, along with my teammates, who had received my constant pounding for every loss. Let's just say I wasn't invited to the team party.

I did meet a special person whose presence around me made me forget my fears. She would hold my hand, and I would melt. These feelings that I never felt before were overwhelming me with happiness. If this is what love was supposed to feel like, I guess I was in love. But that never happened either.

Two weeks before I was supposed to graduate high school, I enlisted into the military. My fears had overtaken me. The future for me was to go serve this country, and the country would take care of me. I was told I wasn't an American until I served my country. School was finished, the foster family was gone, and my family was gone; I thought the only thing I had was this special person, and together we could plan to marry after my military service. But that would never happen. Rather, she wrote me a "Dear John" letter while I was serving in Vietnam. Now she was gone also. Yes, I went to war; I didn't know anything about it and was very naive.

I also was very naive about everything that occurred behind my back as a minor. When my adoptive mother passed away, the lawyer who was in charge of everything, who put me in foster care, and later told me about the family who backed out of the agreement to care for me, also told me of properties my adoptive mother left, which were sold without my knowledge for taxes owed; that's what I was told. The lawyer who had power of attorney over me and all my adoptive mother's properties, I'm sure, took advantage of an opportunity, considering I was just a stupid Indian boy. He left me with nothing but lies.

It is now forty-six years later. I could never make sense of why, if something could go wrong, it would, and I never built up my hopes in any aspect of my life because I knew something would interfere, and usually for the negative not the positive; it's just the way things went. I interpreted this as the curse that came back from the war with me.

The first time its ugly presence was felt was the day I was spit on, but really, I guess the first time I sensed it was on our final retreat in Vietnam. This was the stage the war was in, getting everyone out, except for the defenseless people whose country was lost, not by us, but by the 1972 Congress and Senate of this country who voted to stop aid to Vietnam. I recall looking into the eyes of an old weathered grandmother sitting helpless against her hut, huddled into a ball. I saw anger, fear, and tears poured down her cheeks; she was completely exhausted. I stood there, and my vision became blurred. I felt as though I was looking through orange colored paper; then I saw it, the curse. I was looking at flashes of all the injustices by barbarians of every culture through history, and I was part of it. Just as the soldiers who expelled the Native Americans out of North America, this defeated grandmother might as well have been a part of my culture that had been defeated.

As an artillery soldier, all missions were dependent upon people called Forward Observers (FO), who directed all artillery rounds that killed thousands of whom I presumed were the enemy, since we couldn't see them. Since all FOs were rotated from jungle to mountain firebases, one group observed my gun section and watched how my gun section operated when the missions came in for support. It wasn't until later that my Radio Tech Operator (RTO) informed me that these guys directed our rounds into innocent villages.

The enemy would take cover in these villages, and rather than ceasing fire, they directed the rounds into these villages, killing everyone. Many people had died due to the decisions of these guys, who used our artillery guns to justify their anger toward the Vietnamese people. Yes, it has been forty-six years, and I can still feel the weight of shame and disgust for what occurred. The curse had embodied anyone involved in that disgrace of human life. Coming to this United States, I was given the best education and opportunity to achieve whatever goals I wanted, so when I volunteered to fight for the people of Vietnam for their freedom, I didn't know we were the bad guys. Never had so many people been violated, physically, mentally, and sexually.

I've tried every way to be successful in life, but like always, call it bad luck, it never happened. My daughter was five months pregnant, and my granddaughter would have been the only child to carry the Apache Indian bloodline, but unfortunately, she did not make it. I guess it was not meant to be. Was it the curse punishing me, my daughter asked. Did I sell sold my soul to the devil? It sure felt like it. The flashbacks of the enemy over taking the firebase like ants, retreating to the last stand; the Da Nang Airport, with no planes to escape in, no weapons to fight with, and no way out. The sparks of bullets in the firefight across the airstrip by the South Vietnamese Army, which would fall, and did. The curse had won. We all waited for our deaths. But just like a movie, there was the sound of a plane breaking through the blackness of night, dropping its landing gear and heading right for the enemy. You could see the sparks hitting the side of the C-130 transport as it turned toward us, but it wasn't stopping. It dropped its rear ramp and someone shouted to run for it. As we lifted, we could see the sparks where we were. The Da Nang Airport had fallen, and that's how we departed the war; but so did the curse. It also jumped on board and followed all of us back to the world, where it affected every vet differently. I've done the best I could in readjusting when I came back, but I've lost more than I won. If I continue to wake up each day sucking air, then it's a good day, just like the day I was born.

You never know what each day will bring. Still today I look at each day as an adventure. You can only control the things you can control. I learned to express the truth. Then I realized something; the heavy shame was lifted. The curse couldn't handle the truth, so I wrote it down for everyone to read.

I had wanted to write this story for so many years, but shame and the curse kept stomping me down. It took away my dignity, my self-esteem, my self-worth, and it makes you dysfunctional in life, especially when people spit on you. I can still feel the spit on my face, and it's been forty-three years ago. I'm still surviving, only by the will of God.

The loved ones lost during my era in Vietnam would have probably been around the same age as me. They probably would have children and grandchildren, I assume. Today, we're all dealing with the same issues. Today, people are angry that there's no justice. I would feel the same if I lost a loved one to injustice and the judicial system would declare it justified.

Today, people protest in a peaceful manner, but truthfully, deep inside, they're burning mad with anger. You see, the Vietnam vets back then in the sixties were responsible for the protesting they did. Back then, we were called murderers, baby killers, drug addicts, scum.

All those educated college minds didn't have the guts to serve this country. They didn't even have the college mind to research the five presidential administrations that lied to the people of this country about Vietnam, starting with Truman and continuing with Eisenhower, Kennedy, Johnson, and Nixon. The never did their homework.

Jane Fonda was able to hang out in Hanoi and bad-mouthed those fighting to survive in the south of Vietnam. People like John McCain, who was captured as a prisoner of war, was given the opportunity to go home only out of respect from the North Vietnamese administration due to the fact he was the son of a very well-respected US admiral. His injuries were due to his plane crashing, not torture. The North Vietnamese wanted to send him to the United States of America. My, my, my, what a political opportunity in store for the future, and possibly political career, politician coming from a high-caliber family.

Back then, protesting was just another reason to get drunk, get high, have sex with anyone and everyone; you remember Free Love. And the rich families were able to keep their sons out of harm's way by avoiding Vietnam. If they did go, they worked for the newspaper or as an office jockey of some sort.

I came from a different country. I wasn't born in this United States. My ancestors were pushed out of this country so their land could be stolen. Ancestors of others were brought here as slaves, only to benefit the rich and powerful. I enlisted just as others did, to fight for this country.

I never had a father, but I observed the fathers during the Vietnam era and how they treated their sons by yelling at them to get a haircut, get a job, get out of the house "you low life." Mothers, wives, and daughters were treated the same by being told what to do and taking the physical and mental abuse of being controlled. This was no different than how women were treated in the past. Where was justice?

You're told how awful the Middle Eastern man behaves by controlling their families with women and girls having to cover up or be stoned to death. How long did it take for women in this country to obtain equality, the right to vote, freedom of choice, and still today, women get paid less than men. Where is justice?

Fathers would tell their sons, "When I was your age, I was fighting a war for my country." So were we, but we did not have any support from our country. There was no coalition of nations for support. When we came back, there was no homecoming, just spit and rejection. Where was justice?

I'm setting the tone as to the feelings your lost loved ones were at in this stage of the Vietnam War, which led up to the incident that occurred. Remember the general in charge over there requested 240,000 more troops to finish and obtain victory in Vietnam? Well, to make a long story short, Congress denied the aide to Vietnam, which denied the solider his supplies to fight.

This is when I, and your lost loved ones, was chosen to become members of a task force called Gimlet. A gimlet is the very point of an arrowhead, usually going forward. Not this time. We were selected to be the last ones out and possibly not making it out alive. We were the last combat unit to depart from the Republic of South Vietnam. Had your loved one made it back, they would have been stereotyped as losers, dysfunctional, and moving from home to home, never finding peace.

In my path of life, it's been forty-three years, and the curse still continues. I don't want to carry in my mind that maybe you all were not told the truth. The curse has to be expelled. The curse is carried by every Vietnam veteran that experienced or saw the immoralities of the Vietnam War. From following orders that were inhumane and wrong to the Vietnamese people, or to all the soldiers who did unspeakable acts to as many little girls and boys they could; things they could not do in this United States.

I have a hard time accepting a fellow vet saying they did two or three tours of duty in Vietnam. The truth is that if you could get away with murder, you would. If you could get away with rape, you would. If you could violate a child, you would; but not in these United States. In my Vietnam War experience, I didn't need two or three tours of duty, one was enough.

I'm going to tell you finally what actually happened. There's not a day that goes by that I don't remember. Your loved ones hooked up with one of the best and tightest units, the Americal division. You see, they were infantry, what we called grunts; we were artillery, and called canon cockers. Their support was never-ending for our firebases, which at that stage of the war; we were losing them one right after the other. You have to remember all the ones here were the last combat unit, but of course, you should have known this.

The Americal Division was out in front. Their job was to slow down the enemy, get back to the firebase, where together, the canon cockers and grunts put down some incredible firepower. We fought well together, and I had a lot of respect for them. You must remember, the firebase was the last outpost. The Americal unit moved to all firebases for support. Everything was bad as we were losing firebases, having started with sixteen.

I can't tell you what your loved ones had seen or experienced, but I can tell you the day they escorted, by orders, an entire village of old men, women, children, and animals to a firebase that we were abandoning. The people thought that this was the best for their village. Whoever gave the order to leave the generator with plenty of fuel to give the village light at night made it more enticing to stay, but also made them a target.

I couldn't tell you how many missions they had to deal with, but this mission, we both saw. We hurried to pack up our artillery gun, at the same time trying to tell these people not to stay here. Number 10, which meant *very bad, go back,* but they didn't listen because there was too much excitement. What made me so angry was that someone gave that order. To set up all these people to be killed, slow down the enemy by making it look like Americans were still in the firebase.

After moving to the last remaining firebase, everything fell apart. It was the end, and everyone knew it. Now we all also knew we were fighting for our lives. So now, from the beginning, this is what happened.

Blackness over the jungle at 3,500 feet coming onto an outpost called firebase.

"Fire mission, fire mission!" shouted the CO. "Battery adjust! Azimuth 56! Shell H-E! Two-by-two jack-in-the-box! Charge six! Deflection 4699! Quadrant 689!"

"Ten more rounds, shell H-E now!" shouted the section chief.

Man, wish I was at jack-in-the-box; only thing in twos that I'd be ordering would be burgers, shakes, fries, tacos, and onion rings—yes, yes, yes.

"Gun one, adjust!" shouted the section chief.

"That's us. Gun one, Willie, Peter. Two-by-two jack-in-the-box! Ditto on the Azimuth, deflection and quadrant! Charge Six. Ten Willie Peters now!" shouted the section chief.

Damn, all this gunpowder sure smells good. Mosquitos gotta be flying high. I sure am, damn!

"Coming up on one hundred rounds!" yelled Fox. Fox was our RTO man (radio technician operator). "Cease-fire, cease-fire, mission accomplished!"

Silence covered the whole mountain. Everyone was collapsing on the ground or on a gun. My whole body was pumping like crazy. In the silence, you could hear the mosquitoes breathing. "Throw me a cigarette, gunner." There was nothing like a Kool after a fire mission. The smoke from the gunpowder lingered like fog hanging heavy.

"Red eye, red eye!" shouted Fox. Morning was already here. Damn, I didn't get any sleep; time to get up.

My mind began flashing memories of how I got here. *You volunteered for this remember, remember, remember…* Sixteen months earlier at Fort Sills, Oklahoma; home of the 34 Field Artillery. There were eight weeks of training on the duties of the gun bunnies, damn!

"Welcome, gun bunnies. My name is Sergeant Precott, and I will be your drill instructor for the next eight weeks. You will know and fire every type of Howitzer cannon. You will know what a fire mission is and what your duties will be as a gun bunny! You will be a gun bunny until you pass all fire missions. Then, and only then, will you be called a cannon cocker. But before anyone of you put a hand on my Howitzers, you will have classroom time. Now, I want all of you gun bunnies to follow the specialist so you can be assigned barracks!"

"Listen up, my name is Specialist Anderson. There will be twenty gun bunnies per barracks. You choose the barracks and also the bunks. I guess by now you realize it's rather hot in Oklahoma this time of year. You will also see that we have air conditioners for your convenience. We have two large fans in each barracks. You also will be issued an extra cover blanket for your bunks. Maintenance has removed all outside screens for repairs, which had allowed these tiny black bugs to move in. They don't think they bite, but if they do, blame maintenance. Chow is at 17:00 hours, dismissed!"

Returning from chow, every bunk was covered with bugs. We were all told we better keep all windows shut. After shaking all out extra cover blankets outside and closing the door and windows, the barracks turned into an oven. We turned on the fans, giving us hot air. Oh well, better than bugs.

"Everybody, up!" screamed the specialist. "It's 0500 hours. You gun bunnies have lots of learning to get done today. You have one hour to eat, so let's get moving!"

"Okay, gun bunnies, listen up," said Sergeant Precott. "When you leave here in eight weeks, you will be heading to your permanent party station. Permanent party means you will have, just like civilians, a forty-hour workweek, guard duty or kitchen police does not change, nor will it change anywhere. So check the duty roster to see if you have any duties after today. But before anyone of you receives permanent party, you will know every step to a fire mission and each duty of the seven men who operates a Howitzer! You also will be able to set up and fire every type of Howitzer, understand?"

"Yes, sir," replied the trainees.

"I am not a sir!" screamed Sergeant Precott. "I work for a living, understand? I can't hear you!"

"Yes, Drill Sergeant!"

"I do not want any gun bunny saying 'but I was never taught that' when he gets to permanent party. So let's get started with who the seven men are. Gunner, assistant gunner, number one man, number two man, number three man, number four man, radio technician operator. Everybody understand?"

"Yes, Drill Sergeant!" screamed the trainees.

"The gunner," added the Sergeant, "works with deflection, which means from side to side. The assistant gunner, or AG, works with the quadrant, which means up and down. The number 1 man loads the projectile into the breach of the Howitzer. The number 2 man along with the numbers 3 and 4 men work together in getting the type of projectile, the charge called for and fuse setting and, most important of all, getting the projectile to the number 1 man. The RTO, or radio technician operator, is your call-by-call man. He receives all information from FDC, or fire direction center. He then relays the deflection to the gunner, the quadrant to the assistant gunner, type of round, what charge, and the fuse setting to the numbers 2, 3, and 4 men. The section chief runs the gun pit and must oversee all operations before firing the Howitzer. Now listen to what a fire mission is supposed to sound like!"

"Fire mission, fire mission! Gun 1 adjust."
RTO: Azimuth 100. Two-by-two jack-in-the-box. Shell HE. Deflection 3699!
Gunner: Deflection 3699.
RTO: Quadrant 289.
AG: Quadrant 289.
RTO: Charge six, time fuse 2.5.
Man 3 and 4: Charge six, time fuse 2.5.
AG: Ready to fire!
Chief: Fire!

"Did anybody not understand anything about the fire mission?" asked Sergeant Precott.

"Yes," replied the trainee, "this gun bunny did not understand the two-by-two jack-in-the-box."

The sergeant replied, "A two-by-two jack-in-the-box is ten projectiles, two rounds per deflection and quadrant until all ten rounds are fired, anything else?"

"Yes," again replied the trainee, "the gun bunny did not understand Shell HE."

The sergeant answered, "Shell HE is the type of projectile. H-E stands for high explosive, and WP stands for white phosphorus. Illumination means "give me light," and smoke stands for a marker round, anything else?"

Again the trainee replied, "The gun bunny did not understand charge six or time fuse setting."

"The projectile comes in three sections," replied Sergeant Precott. "A fuse, the projectile, and canister. The fuse comes in two types, impact or timed fuse. The timed fuse is just like an alarm clock, spin to set at whatever is called for. The canister, or the bottom part of the projectile, comes with seven bags of gunpowder. If the mission calls for charge six, then remove the last bag. If it calls for charge five, then remove the last two bags, and so on. You then put the projectile back together and hand it over to the number 1 man, understand?"

"Yes, Drill Sergeant!" shouted the trainees.

"Now," he continued, "for the rest of the day, get into seven-man groups and practice each of the duties of the seven men. Carry on!"

It was the hottest time of the year, and for eight weeks, we drilled and drilled, mission after mission, firing every type of Howitzer cannon, until we were no longer called gun bunnies, but cannon cockers.

Then came the transfer to Fort Lewis, Washington. Fort Lewis, Washington, was home of the 54th Field Artillery, the permanent party station. It was finally here, and how I waited for this day. I was assigned to a mobile track unit, which was just like tanks but quicker; forty-hour workweek, here I was.

"Gentlemen," responded the captain. "I am your commanding officer. You are now part of the 54 Field Artillery. You will be assigned to a gun section and will be expected to carry out the duties of artillery men. Report to the assigned barracks, and tomorrow, you will meet your section chiefs, dismiss!"

Once my head hit the pillow, I was out like a light. Having chow and just sitting around was the last thought on my mind. Before I knew it, the CO was flipping on the lights.

"Everybody, up!" he shouted. "Five o'clock, formation at zero six hundred hours!"

"Welcome to the 54th. I am your section chief. You are going to be in my gun section, gun number 4. We have a good gun crew, so do not hesitate to ask questions. You will have every opportunity to do every job on the one-five-five SP track, even drive it. Come on, the crew is already at the motor pool, that's where we park the guns."

Just thinking about driving the one-five-five SP excited my blood, even to drive the cargo carrier also.

"Everyone, over here," said the chief. "This is our new gun member, let's show him around. I have a section chief's meeting to go to, so carry on."

"Welcome, gun 4," said gunner. "Let me show you around. Okay, guys, let's get back to maintaining the gun and cargo carrier."

"What fort did you train at?"

"Fort Sills, Oklahoma, home of the 34th."

"I went through there," replied gunner. "Damn was it hot, and the mosquitoes ate me up alive out on field training. Sure glad I made it. This place will be paradise to you. I know you were trained on the one-five-five split trails, and do you remember carrying all those one-hundred-pound rounds? Well, here you do not. Everything is done by hydraulics, and all the rounds are inside the 155 SP, plus you get to ride, how about that?"

Well, I did get to ride and drive both the 155 SP and the cargo carrier. Not only that but was also gunner, assistant gunner, number 1, 2, 3, 4, and radio man. Not only did I perform all the duties of an artillery man, but you would not believe all the maintenance it took to keep these monsters running. From changing track pads to changing oil to replacing engines; for a while, I thought I was a grease monkey.

Three to four months went by, and doing the same routines were now getting to me. The field training at Fort Sills was hot, now the field training in Washington was freezing my butt off. I desperately needed a change. I would take anything; at least on guard duty or kitch police, I had the next day off.

I heard that headquarters needed volunteers for honor guard burial detail. What the hell, why not go for it? At least it would keep me out of field training. They sure sucked, so what if the honor guard was burial detail. At least I would get to travel all over Washington state.

Staying at the Holiday Inns or whatever hotels were close was now paradise; good food, warm rooms. What more could a person ask for? Most of the time after burial ceremonies, we had off, and at that time, our concentration was on how good we were having it. I could really start to enjoy doing this. Yes, sir, this was the good life.

We were sharp from carrying the caskets to folding the flag, to our twenty-one-gun salute with taps finishing. We took pride in our honor guard, but after numerous burials, I started to see beyond our pride and into the faces of the people who lost their fathers, sons, and husbands. I then realized that these men were killed in Vietnam. They gave their lives for what they thought was right. I was evidently worried about freezing my butt off and complaining about every lit-tle thing that didn't go right. I kept asking myself, did all these dead men have a choice? Well, it's too late to ask them, but not too late for me. I just had to find out for myself.

When the honor guard returned to Fort Lewis, I went ahead and applied for a transfer. A transfer to where? You got it, the Republic of South Vietnam. No sooner were we back that another burial came up. And before we had to leave, we learned that a levy for Germany and Korea had arrived at Fort Lewis. I wondered what destination my orders were for, and Korea sounded better than Germany. Guess I have to find out when I returned back to the fort again. For now, there were just two more burials first.

It was night when we returned back to Fort Lewis. Sleep sounded too good. I could not wait to get into the barracks. "Hey, what is going on, where is everyone?" I said. The barracks was empty. "Just three out of thirty people are left?" I asked. "Hey, Jones, where are you headed, Germany or Korea?"

"You are the last one left, dude. My orders are for Germany," he said. "And so are theirs, with a thirty-day leave for home first. We are out of here, good luck."

"Yeah, later, good luck, bed is where I'm headed since I'm the only one left."

Morning came too early. I felt like I just went to sleep, damn. Just then the barracks doors flung open, entering the CO who said, "Your orders are down in the captain's office. See you down there later."

Saturday morning, and it figures, it was my day off. I better get up and go see where I was headed. "Well, where are they?" I asked.

"I did not think you would be too long. Want a drink of Madd Dog 20/20?" the captain asked.

"They cannot be that bad. So what if I got Germany, hand them over to me so I can see," I stated.

"Just sit down, let me break it down to you so you can under-stand them," he said.

"I can read, now give them here."

"Yeah well," he shouted, "I was there, so now just listen! The following individual must start processing procedures, departing Fort Lewis, Washington, and proceed en route to Da Nang City, Republic of South Vietnam."

"I'll take that drink of Madd Dog 20/20 now!" I stated.

"I don't know why only you got these orders. I was there, and if you have any questions, ask."

"I volunteered for it," I told him, "but I didn't think they would listen to me."

"Well," he said, "here's your proof. You regret it now?"

"No," I told him. "I still feel the same about it. I have to find out for myself."

Tiger Airlines flew us to Da Nang City. Nineteen hours; there must have been three hundred newbies getting off that afternoon. The air was hot and tropical. Everyone was marched into a large airstrip hangar. Planes and choppers were parked inside. I guess they were getting worked on for a mission. As we stood there, the silence was broken by a staff sergeant screaming out, "I need twelve volunteers right now to be chopper door gunners. I should also tell you that the life of a door gunner is at the most three months!"

At least he was honest about it, but I would like to live a little longer than three months or so. Again he screamed out, "I want everyone into the buses outside. They will take you all to the LZ Red Horse, from there, you will be assigned to your units. Dismiss!"

Funny thing about those buses, steel mesh and steel bars covered all the windows. Sure made us feel like prisoners, especially when two army jeep escorts, each mounted with dual M-50 caliber machine guns, one in the front of the bus and the other bringing up to rear, sped us through the streets of the city.

Going through the streets of Da Nang City, I could feel the hatred from the people as they stopped what they were doing to look at us. I felt more comfortable as I saw the entrance to LZ Red Horse. Inside, I was puzzled when I noticed an area that we went by that was fenced off like a prison with posted guards. But all the men who I noticed walking around inside the fenced area wore hospital robes, and everyone had massive hair loss, in chunks. Strange, I thought, but whatever they had, I didn't want.

We were assigned barracks for the night, but like everyone else, we were too edgy and curious; everything looked so different. We were told to keep away from the perimeter wire. Like I really wanted to go near where snipers were spotted across the rice paddies. We were also shown where to go if we were to receive incoming fire. That did it; no way were we going to get any sleep. Funny thing through. neither did any of the old-timers. Strange feeling that was, going through the day, continuing into the night, and through the next day, and never acknowledging it; time had ceased to exist. Sunrises were welcomed with big heavy sighs that I did notice. The mess hall had breakfast ready, but we could not eat; made sense why returning vets to the world looked very different as to when they first got there.

Units were being assigned. I, along with some others, was told to report to the armory for weapons issue, along with ammo. Now my blood started to boil. My heart pounded even more when we were told to get our gear, report to the landing pad to get onto the chopper that called out your given number; mine was Maude-350. I was dazed, and I could feel the sweat running down my back clear down to my ass. All I could think was *350, Maude, chopper, gear, weapon,* and *ammo.* Oh god, I'm talking in circles.

Then the sounds of the choppers seemed to pop right out of the air like a big, big wind storm. All four choppers moved in perfect motion. The door gunners jumped out of all four choppers and ran toward us, screaming out numbers: *2001! 1751! 300! 2501!*

I was so taken by the approach, I almost forgot my number until the door gunner was yelling 350 right in front of me. *Here I go.* I waited too long getting on the chopper. The only seat left was on the floor near the door. I thought the door would be slid shut but soon realized what door? As the chopper started to bank, my butt became one strong suction cup, and I was not lying either!

What a view of Vietnam from up here. One beautiful country with everything so green, so wet, so jungle, and the rice paddies just never seemed to end. Seemed like we'd been flying for hours, then the door gunner pointed to the north, but all we could see was a brown spot in the distance. I did notice that the paddy fields started to take strange shape, but then realized those strange shapes were craters from artillery rounds that exploded. Now the brown spot had gotten bigger, and as we started to circle, I could see the gun pits, six of them all were one-o-deuces Howitzers. Was this my unit? I had a strong indication it was; this was going to be home.

As we touched down, the door gunner gave us the thumbs-up, and we returned it. No sooner than we were out, the chopper was off. I suddenly felt stranded on top of a mountain with Charlie below, damn!

"All newbies over here and fall in!" screamed Smoke.

"Gentlemen," replied the Captain. "I'm your commanding officer, and I want to welcome you to Firebase Maude, Hill 350. You now belong to the 196th Light Infantry Brigade and are part of the third of the Eighty-Second Field Artillery. We have six-gun pits, and you will be assigned to one of them to carry out your duties as artillery men. As you can see, there's no way off this firebase except by chopper, so unless you can sprout wings, we'll depend on each other until the very end. Then we'll all go home in body bags. That's all, and welcome aboard. Smoke, assign these men to a gun pit," said the captain.

"Grab your gear and follow me. As you can see, I'm your first sergeant, but you can call me Smoke."

"Smoke!" shouted a section chief. "I'm short one man, help me out."

"You're in luck, Chief," replied Smoke. "I just happen to have an extra. Drop your gear, newbie, and welcome to your gun pit."

"I'm your section chief, welcome to gun pit 1. What's your name, newbie?" asked the section chief. Once I told him,_Micheal Hall, he screamed at me, "Don't screw with me!" And asked me again. "So we both have the same name, huh? Well, what's your middle name?" When I told him, he said, "Well who's going to get killed first, newbie, A before R or R before A? Gun 1, fall in. New man on board," screamed the section chief.

"This here is your gunner, and this is your assistant gunner. This here is the number 1 man until I decide different. Here is the charge and fuse man, and here's your call-by-call radio man. But you have the most important job of all," replied Chief. "You're my ammo man, and it's OJT, on the job training. RTO will show you where to put your gear. We live in holes just big enough for your body. Tomorrow we'll help dig yours. If any missions come up, you just listen up and bring the ammo. Watch what we do and keep your head down. It's all self-explanatory."

"How long have you been in country?" asked RTO.

"Three days, how about yourself?"

RTO responded, "six months and two firebases."

"What happened to the two firebases?" I asked.

RTO responded again, "Well, we had to evacuate kind of quickly, Charlie wanted that mountain real bad so we let him have it, we booby-trapped it, then left it. Six Chinook choppers picked up all six guns and flew us across the valley. We set up and fired two hundred rounds per gun on top. Once we knew he was on top. Sure was beautiful, just beautiful."

"Listen," he said, "my apartment isn't any wider than the other guys, it's just a little longer, gotta have leg room you know. You can bed down near the entrance, chow should be here soon. Grab beanie weenies if you can, it's one of the best for C rations."

"Right now I could use some sleep. I think jet lag is catching up to me," I, the newbie, replied.

My eyes felt like they were on fire. Three days without sleep, and it was hard keeping them open. Closing them was my first mistake.

"Fire mission, fire mission! Get up, get up!" screamed RTO.

"What, what, damn, okay, okay where am I, damn?" I mumbled to myself.

"Fire mission, fire mission, gun 1 adjust!" screamed Chief. "Azimuth 39!"

RTO cut in, "Five rounds, shell HE. Charge six, time fuse, 3.5."

Number 4 man cut in, "Charge six, time fuse 3.5."

RTO came back, "Deflection 1462."

Gunner came back, "Deflection 1462."

RTO cut in, "Quadrant 689."

AG came back, "Quadrant 689. Ready to fire!"

Chief took over. "Hold your fire!"

While waiting for all guns to adjust, I was impressed with how quick our gun pit was. I wondered who was in trouble, who was calling it in? How close was Charlie to them? Suddenly I heard over the radio, "Fire!"

I must have jumped a foot off the ground. Our gun pit pumped out those five rounds just like a repeating rifle. The thunder, cracking, and shaking of the ground was something else against the blackness of night.

RTO suddenly shouted out, "Cease-fire, cease-fire, mission accomplished!"

"Good job, men," commended Chief. "Let's pick up the gun pit and put back the five rounds in the ammo bunker. Gunner, rotate the perimeter guard and give my new ammo man the layout for guard duty," he continued.

"What time is it anyway, gunner?" I asked.

Gunner replied, "0400 hundred hours, time to get up. This is guard bunker number 7, memorize each object inside and where it lays. At night, you can't see your hands in front of your face, let alone the M-60 machine gun, hand grenades, ammo for the M-60, the kacker triggers that go with the claymores, and the most important item, the radio."

"When do I go on guard duty?" I asked.

"Tonight at twenty-four-hundred hours, with me," he remarked.

Suddenly Chief screamed out, "Fire mission, fire mission, battery adjust."

Everyone was making mad dashes for their gun pits. They looked like ants crawling over everything and anything. It was a mad house the rest of the day. I'd never carried so much ammo. And RTO was right. When the C-rations came, beanie weenies were the first to go. You had to be quick on the first grab. Time went by so fast that I missed it.

"You stay with RTO again," replied Chief, "since we didn't get to your hutch today. Tomorrow is another day. Gunner, check the rotation on the perimeter, set out all claymores, and take the newbie with you," he added.

"Grab that bag and follow me," Gunner said. "Make sure you step where I step, we have the whole side of this mountain boo-by-trapped. Inside the bag you're carrying, there's six claymores and blasting caps. We're going to place them at equal distances in front of gun one's guard bunker. We also have fifty feet of fuse that, after attaching them to the claymores, we will run up to the bunker and attach them to the kackers, understand? Each kacker and each claymore must have the same number. We have a saying up here that if after an overrun of the firebase by Charlie, we find you dead with a stupid look on your face, then we know that Charlie was up on your right and the kacker you squeezed went off on your left. Tomorrow night, you'll be doing this by yourself, so watch close."

"How close does Charlie get anyhow?" I asked.

Gunner responded, "We've found guys in the morning sitting inside their guard dead. Does that answer your question? Just because we have bigger guns doesn't mean we're the winners. Remember, we can't shoot downhill, but we do have a little present for Charlie when he does come over the top."

Gunner walked over to the ammo bunker, lifted the tarp, and patted two HE rounds that read *Beehive*. "Inside each one of these babies"—he smirked—"are a million one-inch steel arrows. You slap this puppy inside the gun, lower the tube to waist level, wait for Charlie to be in perfect range, and let him have it. Remember, this round has a time fuse setting for two or three seconds, so it's going to go off right in front of you. Anything or anybody in front will be stripped clean to the bone!"

Suddenly the Chief shouted out, "Fire mission, fire mission, battery adjust."

Here we go again; fire missions were never ending. Time was sure flying by. The noise was deafening, and before you knew it, damn, it was morning already. The medic appeared out of nowhere and said, "I need gun 1's shit-burning detail personnel, ASAP."

"Sorry, newbie," said Chief, "but you're bottom man on the list, so go with Doc."

"Follow me," Doc remarked, "I have two more gun pits to visit."

"What's shit-burning detail anyways?" I asked.

"It's one detail," he added, "that everyone has to do at one time or another. So don't feel bad about it. It has to be done."

"What has to be done?" I asked.

"Well," he started, "you know the shit houses. Each container has to be pulled out, making sure no one is using it, then emptied into a diesel container mixed with gas. It's started on fire and stirred. That's how we get the term *shit burning detail*. If we didn't do this, we would all be sick. Maybe some would die from the diseases.

"No," he continued. "We can't just dump it over the side of the mountain or bury it. The diseases would still get to all of us. I won't stop you all from any cussing, swearing, or upchucking, just grit your teeth and hold your breath. But I will give you a piece of advice, the army's gas mask that you were issued works real good. So let's get moving. We have seven shit houses to do. Each contains four containers. That's twenty-eight piles of shit to burn, so let's move it!"

This definitely was not a motivating job. If you went too fast, shit would splash all over, and if you went too slowly, the heavier it was holding those containers while emptying them. Plus you had to hold your breath, damn!

Doc came back saying, "Good job, guys, now just remember, the next time you use the outhouses and it's shit burning detail, you've already done it, hahaha!"

As I came back to the gun pit, Chief saw me and shouted, "Over here, newbie—phew, never mind. I see and smell that you tried to go too fast on shit-burning detail. AG, take the newbie and show him the showers and how to work them, now!"

"I did the same thing," AG said, "when I was a newbie, and so did a lot of other guys, so don't think you're the first. Here, get inside the stall and start stripping. I'll start the heater to the water tank, so watch what I'm doing. Each person after each shower must refill whatever amount of diesel for the heat they used, plus add two five-gallon cans of water back into the water tank. I'll do it for you this time only."

Just then, Chief came shouting, "Fire mission, fire mission, battery adjust! Shell Willie Peter!"

"Hey!" I screamed. "What am I supposed to do?"

"Grab your pants and get over to the gun pit now!" he yelled.

"Over here, newbie!" screamed Chief. "Take over as number 1 man, let's pump out these rounds!"

He wasn't kidding when he said pump out these rounds, damn. When were these missions going to stop? My arms felt like they were going to explode. Just then, RTO screamed out, "Cease-fire, cease-fire! Mission accomplished."

"Good job, newbie," said Chief. "I'm impressed. You sure can load this gun faster than anyone I've seen so far. You're going to be my number 1 man."

"Chief!" screamed the CO. "FDC just received radio report from the unit that called for the support and said that whoever's gun pit pumped out those rounds so fast just saved their butts and wanted to say thanks a lot!"

Chief shouted back, "I've got a new gun loader who can pump out more rounds and load faster than anyone on the base."

"Good," he remarked, "because after tomorrows resupply of ammo, get your gun and men ready. For the next day, your gun pit is to be flown north along with gun 2's pit."

"How many rounds are we taking this time?" asked Chief.

"Two hundred rounds per gun. Better inform your men it's a hot landing zone," he added.

"RTO," called Chief. "Get my new gun loader informed and updated on what's coming down in two days."

"Okay," responded RTO. "Get your M16 and all the ammo you can carry ready. Tomorrow we won't have time when the ammo for the gun is flown in. We'll be busy getting the ammo, all two hundred rounds, for the gun."

"What did the CO mean when we get flown north?" I asked.

"We're going to put straps on the guns along with a net so it will carry the ammo. When everything is secured, a Chinook chopper will land, letting all of us aboard. They'll lift up again and move over the gun where Chief will hook the gun to the belly of the chopper. Then picking everything up, we'll start our field trip north." He smirked. "A hot landing zone," he continued, "means what it says. We'll have both guns, just enough time to pump out four hundred before Charlie locates our position. Then it's back home again. Simple, right? Now, before you start thinking about how everything is going to happen, start writing what we call our last letter home. We never know what will happen out there, or if we'll come back."

I started writing a letter but couldn't stop thinking about our hot landing zone. When I arrived here on this mountain, I felt stranded. Now they were taking two guns and fourteen men, flying us up north to who knows where, dropping both guns off, shooting our ammo, and praying for a return pick-up before Charlie picked us off. If that's not being stranded, then I don't know what is!

I just wrote back home and more or less told them that if they didn't hear from me in two weeks, something happened to the mission, but hopefully, I told them, I would write as soon as we returned. I then realized with all the confusion going on that I totally forgot to shower after shit-burning detail, damn! I couldn't get to the shower fast enough, hoping I could get through the shower without one fire mission.

As I finished showering, Chief saw me headed back to the hutch and shouted, "You're in luck! The man you replaced as number 1 just received his papers home, so you can move into his hutch and call it home."

Later, RTO popped his head inside the hutch saying, "Chief told me about your new home, so I brought over your gear. Hey, you have lots of room in here, but that only means more rats."

"What do you mean more rats?" I asked.

"I guess you haven't had time to spot them." He smirked. "But now that you have your own hole, you'll see what I mean."

Then Chief popped his head in shouting, "Fire mission, fire mission, let's go. We're going to be firing all night!"

Damn, Chief wasn't kidding. It was the morning already, and time sure did fly over here. The only thing on my mind now was on the hot landing zone and when the Chinook choppers were going to arrive.

"Gun 1!" shouted Chief. "Get your gear and be ready to board a Chinook when it gets here in five minutes, and double-check the ammo net so it won't get tangled during lift-off."

"Chinooks at nine o'clock!" shouted Gunner.

"Gun 1!" yelled Chief. "Grab your gear and head for the landing pad."

"Chief!" yelled the CO. "The first Chinook is yours, get your men aboard. I'll get Smoke to hook up your gun."

Everyone's blood was now really pumping. You could see the excitement in their eyes. These Chinooks could really stir up some dust, and if you didn't hold on to your helmet, it would be gone—and I mean *gone*.

The back section of the Chinook chopper dropped down like a trapdoor, and in we went. No sooner than we were inside, the trapdoor was rising up behind us. We started lifting up and moving over our gun pit. We could see Smoke standing on top of the gun with the hooking straps in his hands. These choppers created such strong winds that trying to hook the straps and keeping your balance was a job in itself. But Smoke succeeded after five attempts at the belly hook then up and off the firebase we went with gun 2 right behind us. It seemed like we had been flying for hours, looking through the belly of the chopper; all we could see was jungle and the gun with the ammo net below swaying from side to side. The door gunner signaled to Chief that we were here, and everyone seemed to have a hard time swallowing.

"We're here!" yelled Chief. "The chopper is going to set down the ammo net first then the gun and then us. Get the setup and ready to fire. Gun 2 will be doing the same, let's go."

Once we set up the guns, our mission was to destroy an area used by the North Vietnamese nationals for transporting supplies. When the first round was fired, we knew our position was no longer a secret, and Charlie would be here in no time. In the middle of nowhere, I knew fourteen men without ammo was no match against Charlie.

"RTO!" yelled Chief. "We're down to our last five rounds, call to see if our pick up is underway."

"I've already started," replied RTO. "They should've been here already. I have a bad feeling about this."

"Well, keep on trying," came back Chief. "We've been here way too long."

"Chinooks at six o'clock!" yelled Gunner.

"Head for the chopper and get on!" shouted Chief. "I'll hook up the gun."

AG suddenly started yelling, "Incoming, incoming, Charlie's here!"

He sure was, and none too soon either. They started firing one-twenty-two rockets at us; they were going off everywhere. Both gun sections were making mad dashes for the choppers. Both chiefs were on top of each gun, ready for hook up. We knew that these chopper pilots had strict orders to abort any mission instead of losing the chopper. But not these guys; they moved the Chinooks over the guns where the chiefs were waiting after picking us up so they could hook up. The chiefs themselves were wondering, since the landing zone had turned extremely hot, if the pilots were going to leave them there.

The first try for hookup was successful, and up we went like a rocket, with the chiefs still on top of the guns letting loose on Charlie with his M16. The belly gunner signaled to him to start climbing up until he was through the belly of the chopper. He looked at us and started laughing then said, "Mission accomplished." We all busted out laughing. As we neared the little brown spot in the distance, we all knew it was going to feel good to be back home, as crazy as it was.

"Welcome back," commented the CO. "We heard over the radio about the close call. I see everyone made it. Good. Now let's get back to keeping Charlie off this mountain."

"Gunner!" yelled Chief. "Break out the C rations and make out the perimeter rotation for tonight. The CO. informed me that Gun 1 and Gun 2 are dismissed from any fire missions tonight."

"Hey, newbie," yelled RTO. "You've been inside your hutch yet?"

"No, why?" I asked.

"Remember about the rats? Well, now is a good time to see for yourself. Don't go in yet, just shine the flashlight inside and see those red beady eyes. Those, my friends, are rats. While we were gone, they've been having a picnic. They've been into everything of yours. We have a saying up here, don't jump right into your hutch because the rats here are big enough to put on your boots and kick your butt out. Just make a lot of noise first and then get out of the way, and you'll see them run out like crazy. I'll see you later. I have to go run out my own pets now."

After evicting my tenants from my hutch, sleep was what I needed. I was so tired, and I would save my C rations for later, must have some sleep.

"Fire mission, fire mission!" someone was shouting.

"What, huh, okay, I'm up, damn, it's still night," I mumbled.

"Relax, relax, calm down, we're still off," remarked RTO. "Wake up and get your senses together. Hey, I didn't know you were a momma?"

"What the hell are you talking about?" I asked.

RTO continued, "While you were asleep, lots of momma rats used your body heat to give birth to all kinds of babies. Your body heat acted as an incubator. That's why there's an imprint on your body made from newborns on your cot. Just brush them off outside, you can't stop them, not unless you plan on never going to sleep."

"All right you two," said Chief suddenly. "Just because you have a day off, doesn't mean you can go brain dead."

"What's coming down, Chief?" RTO asked.

"If you look up," he answered, "you'll see what's coming down. That's a monsoon heading this way, and we're right in its path. This is surely Charlie's weather."

"I'll go get the rest of the gun section," replied RTO.

"What for Chief?" I asked.

"We need to sandbag around the ammo bunkers," he answered, "so the rain doesn't get the gunpowder wet."

"But the ammo bunkers are already two feet off the ground. What? Are we going to flood?" I asked with a smirk.

"Exactly!" he screamed. "Before it's over, which will be in about three weeks or longer, you'll be cussing and swearing at that monsoon! I will tell you this, and you better listen, and listen real good, this is what you call Charlie's weather. Expect him to try to overrun this firebase. He's going to give it his best shot."

"Chief," interrupted Gunner, "all other gun sections are setting out their listening sensors."

"I'll take the gun section and start sandbagging. You take our number 1 man with you and set out the sensors," Chief ordered.

"Where are we going?" I asked Gunner.

"Grab your M16 and follow me," he said. "We have three sensors to set out, just like the claymores."

"What do you want me to do?" I asked.

Gunner took off saying, "I'll set them out, you cover me, then meet me back on top in the bunker.

"Now," he continued back in the bunker. "We test them. Put on the headset. Each sensor has a different number of beeps. I'm going to throw this rock down the hill to your left, tell me how many beeps you hear all together?"

"One," I said.

"Now I'm throwing straight down."

"Two beeps," I replied.

"Now I'm throwing right."

"Three beeps," I continued.

"Good," he said. "They all work!"

"Why haven't we used these babies before?" I questioned.

"How many monsoons have you been through?" he asked.

"This will be my first," I answered.

"Let me straighten you out," he started, "on a few realities. You still think this government will save you even though here you are on top of this forsaken mountain with no support."

"We have all kinds of air support," I came back at him.

"Did you know," he started, "that choppers can't fly in bad monsoons or typhoons. If they can't fly, how are we going to get our support or ammo? Charlie knows this too, and he's going to throw everything at us. Look at the reality of where you are. I don't know, or care, how you got over here, but I'm not here by choice, so arguing won't solve a damn thing. But since I have no choice, and if I'm going to survive like I was trained, then damn it, just like you said earlier, where's the support?"

He continued, "Do you honestly think that our brass leaders in the rear are planning a spearhead operation for us? The only spearhead mission on their minds is in a warm room between the sheets with a couple women! We're on our own up here, so start getting used to it. We live day by day! Now, surviving the elements is another story. It brings out the animal in us. This is where we win as survivors, and it pisses Charlie off! Charlie will crawl a mile up the hill through mud to get us. What he doesn't know is that the survivors on top are no longer human!"

The day finally came when we found out who came first; Michael A before R, or Michael R before A. The CO came to me and said to report to his hutch. As I entered his hutch he said, "Sit down, Specialist. Your section chief requested that you take over a gun pit, so I'm putting you in charge of Gun 6."

"Sir," I said, "I really don't want it. There are others that qualify for that position."

He looked at me and remarked, "I really don't give a shit what you want!"

I said, "Sir, I'm not a sergeant. I'm just a Specialist 4."

He came back at me, "I don't give a shit. You're the only one qualified since you went through the Field Artillery Academy at Fort Sills. I have Sergeant stripes for you here now. Paperwork will come later, and get the hell out of my hutch!"

As I exited his hutch, I could feel the crosshairs zeroing in on me. I could no longer blend in. Rumor had it that all brass had to watch their back if they couldn't blend in. You don't make enemies, if you know what I mean, and that also went for Sergeants.

I entered the gun pit, and Fox yelled out loud, "Gun 6, section chief on board!"

The looks on their faces was one of awe. I yelled out first, "I'm just as surprised as you all!"

The monsoons came and went, and so did our boxer shorts and socks. You couldn't keep them dry, so no one wore any. On came the mud—or, should I say, rivers of mud. We weren't the only ones sitting on sandbagged roofs, and we finally got to see all our hidden pets: spiders as big as the palm of your hand, scorpions with double stingers, bright orange centipedes one inch wide and one foot long, and rats with so many babies that they were clinging to anything.

Life was totally miserable, and it got even worse once Charlie set up two hundred feet down below with the jungle for perfect cover and the monsoons making more perfect camouflage. Charlie was able to shell us with one-twenty-two rockets and having a picnic doing it. While keeping our heads down from incoming fire, Charlie would crawl up the hill until he was inside our perimeter. But one thing Charlie didn't know, and we did, was that Firebase 250 was arranged to give us support and vice versa. It sure was a strange sound: incoming from your own side and hitting your perimeter. But it sure caught Charlie by surprise. We also knew that Firebase 250 couldn't keep up the support. Just like us, their ammo was low, and just like us, they were on their own.

Well, three different firebases later, hot landing zone after hot landing zone, fire mission after fire mission, monsoon after monsoon, section chief after section chief, gunner after gunner, men after men, time after time, I started getting pelted by drops of rain, the sound of lightning brought my thoughts back to the present.

"Chief!" yelled RTO. "Fire mission, fire mission, fire mission. Gun 6, adjust!"

Another damn fire mission; I couldn't remember how many. I told myself that I would keep track of all missions that I would participate in while in Vietnam, but what a joke. I couldn't even tell how many rounds my gun pit fired. Even though I had a logbook to keep track of everything, which Fox, my RTO man, had kept in perfect order, while I watched him receive the mission from the FDC (fire direction center). Fox recorded Azimuth to the gun section, the deflection to the gunner, the quadrant to the assistant gunner, and the type of round and the quantity to the rest of the gun section, while desperately writing it all down in that little green log register book, so as to answer any questions of error from headquarters, for this gun section had already experienced a nightmare that we as a gun pit would never be able to forget.

Red eye, or as some would call it the sun, once again saved us from the terrors of the blackness, which confined us as prisoners on top of this forsaken mountain every night. On this particular day, red eye was at about ten o'clock, and the most spectacular sight never seen by man, was all around the mountain. The only sight that took away from this beautiful setting was the six artillery Howitzers perfectly placed on the crown of the mountain. The feeling was that of the Greek gods on top of Mount Olympus. The war was subconsciously forgotten, the most spectacular formation of clouds, so thick that they actually encircled the top of the firebase, right up to the first trench, which encompassed the mountain; so thick that there was no more earth, just formations of stairs and incredible waterfalls so thick that the urge to step off the mountain onto this illusion was real.

We were above the clouds most of the day. Funny thing though, the day was half gone without one fire mission. How strange. I thought everyone below the clouds was just as lost as we were. There was no visibility as far as the eye could see. The winds started to pick up, and in the distance, the sky was turning black and was heading right for us. The scenery changed as though someone had changed the film up to fast forward. The O's frantic voice broke the trance, and the war was once again in motion.

"Fire mission, fire mission!" yelled Fox. "Chief, Gun 6 ONLY, adjust!" Once again, Fox had beaten the gun section back to the gun pit with his headset on. He was intensely jotting down the mission called from FDC. He looked up, and we locked eyes. As I adjusted my headset, I glanced down at the logbook, and he had already jotted down five two-by-two jack-in-the-box. That's already fifty rounds, but the voice over the radio kept going, adding more rounds and, in between, babbling something about a grunt unit caught in an ambush and needing support as soon as possible.

"Empty all HE bunkers!" I yelled.

"We need time fuses also!" Fox shouted. "Set time fuses at 2.5," he continued. "Stand by, Gun 6," he said. "Azimuth—3500! Deflection—356! Quadrant—5601! Shell—HE! Two-by-two jack-in-the-box! Time Fuse—2.5! Charge—7!"

"Ready to fire!" shouted the Gunner!

"Ready to fire!" shouted AG!
"Stand by, Gun 6!" shouted Fox. "Gun 6, fire!"
"FIRE!" I shouted.

The mission was under way. I could only feel that the only reason for selecting Gun 6 was due to the accuracy and speed Gun 6 operated under, and this certainly was urgent. The other five gun pits were also standing ready. By this time, I could feel the rain starting to fall. These were big raindrops with winds blowing at least ten to fifteen miles per hour. This was surely Charlie's weather.

"Keep the gunpowder dry," I yelled. "Let's go, keep it going."

Observing the whole gun section, I could only feel proud of these men. Their efforts were well over 100 percent, and I was hoping that our support was accomplishing its mission. Observing the gun pit was like looking into the engine of a car when everything was working together with great precision. Every two rounds, Fox would yell out another deflection to the gunner and continue with the quadrant to the assistant gunner, who in turn would fire the Howitzer on my command while the rest of the gun section moved with such accuracy that listening to the gun firing was like listening to the seconds tick on a Timex, not once missing a beat.

In our minds, we could picture the rounds landing. For every deflection, the gun would move just like the second hand of a watch, and for every quadrant, the elevation would change up or down. So in our minds, we could picture the rounds exploding before they hit the ground because of the time fuse. We were achieving air burst explosions, covering a radius of about one quarter of a circumference of a circle; whatever was alive before the explosions was surely terminated after.

Click click click click.

Everyone's head turned toward the AG, and once more he tried.

Click click.

"Jammed round, jammed round!" I shouted. "Clear the gun now!" I yelled. "Get me the extraction tool, Gunner! We have a hot tube, and we have to extract the round before it detonates from the heat. Elevate the gun. AG, open the breech now! Gunner, get ready to catch it. It's going to be hot," I continued.

"Chief, Gunner," Fox started shouting, "get away, it's going to blow, get away, it's too hot!"

Got to get it out, got to get it out. Man, it was hot. The rain then became most obvious because every drop that hit the tube was immediately evaporated, leaving a hissing sound—*sssssss*. Gunner was shaking so much, I was afraid he would drop the round. He couldn't keep his eyes open out of fear it was going to blow up in our faces.

Out of ten rounds in this two-by-two, we jammed on the eighth round. We had to unjam the gun piece to complete the mission.

"It's free!" I yelled.

"Cease-fire, cease-fire, crease-fire!" Fox shouted. "Chief, get on the radio," Fox requested.

"It's FDC!"

"This is Gun 6," I returned.

"Cease-fire, cease-fire," FDC responded. "Gun 6, we have friendly fire, freeze the gun piece!"

"You get down here now!" I shouted. "And you better be joking!" "Gunner," I yelled, "freeze the gun piece!"

Fox had been listening on the other headset. Fox was Caucasian, but when he heard what I just heard, he turned white. I'm not white, but I know at that moment I felt very pale. He instinctively handed me the logbook, which contained the deflections and quadrants of all the missions, which FDC would automatically ask for to compare the data leading up to the last set of deflections and quadrants, which should match up with FDC and the gun.

I knew before they all started toward the gun piece that the numbers of deflection and quadrant for the Gunner and the Assistant Gunner matched with the logbook and also with FDC, so I didn't go with them. I could understand Fox, Gunner, and AG for going, but I had already checked them all before the last round jammed, so I knew everyone matched numbers. My thoughts were on the "friendlies" we just wiped out and who was responsible for calling in the wrong grid, and thank God for the eighth round jamming, or we would have finished firing all ten rounds.

Something changed in the gun pit that night that would affect us all for the rest of our lives.

Though the rain and wind had picked up fiercely, I could see the outline of my gun section, huddled together in front of my hutch. They knew what happened, but to what extreme, or who, was all that was lacking from their own questioning.

"Chief, why is the tube elevated in that position?" FDC questioned.

Fox cut in, "We had a jammed round, number 8, laying over there on the trails, and Chief, Gunner, and AG elevated the tube to extract the jammed round. They left the gun in that position when cease-fire was alerted."

"If you check your data," I started, "along with my RTO's data, for the quadrant on round number 8, you'll find out they all match for that two-by-two mission, and the rest that my specialist has stated is also true."

"Until tomorrow," FDC stated, "Gun 6 is ordered frozen upon further investigation by the inspector general. Gun 6's gun crew will assist the other gun pits until further notice."

It's difficult to say, or even think, the term *friendly fire*. Why did this have to happen to this gun section? Guilt had set in and had taken over the gun crew. Every man was assigned to different gun sections. The hard part about this nightmare that occurred is that every man involved in the mission knew it was not our fault. It didn't make a difference though, and we were branded, divided up, and abandoned.

Two weeks passed, and still no notice of any investigation had been received. And to make matters worse, just as I was about to write back home to my girl, more or less to empty my gut about the accident because I needed a shoulder to cry on, mail call came first. There was a surprise letter from her, and I thought to myself it's just what I needed. But it wasn't, and instead she was asking me for comfort and understanding. To make it short, I received my "Dear John" letter.

What else was headed my way? At this point, I didn't really care. This war certainly was not heading for any glorious victory but instead was heading toward retreat. Morale did not exist, and units were fighting against units, whites were fighting blacks, Mexicans and Puerto Ricans were fighting against everyone, the enlisted against their brass, the regular army against the draftees. Vietnam was falling, and no one could stop it. I felt for the first time the agony of defeat. Where was my country?

I lost my gun pit. I was under investigation for friendly fire kill. My gun section crew had been assigned to different gun pits. Everything fell apart, and I felt empty, not alive, and the fear of being killed was gone; it was what it was!

My girl back home wrote me a "Dear John" letter. I knew her through high school; my only love, and now she didn't want me anymore. I felt dead inside. My plans with her to marry and have a future together were gone. I wished I was dead. *What next* was the thought that raced through my mind. No sooner than I had that thought, the remaining Americal unit that escaped from being killed by friendly fire was hunting down the gun pit responsible for killing their buddies. They formed a semi-circle outside my gun pit, raised their M16s, and "locked and loaded" on me, shouting, "What gun pit is this?"

Fox was behind me, and I turned around and told him to get me a Beehive Round Charge 4, Time Fuse 1.5 seconds. I slammed one Beehive into the gun, dropped the barrel at waist level, and pointed it at them. "You killed our buddies, and we're here for payback!" one shouted. I could hear the click on their M16s, which meant the safety was off.

"You'll kill me," I shouted, "but I'll wipe you all out with this Beehive round." Everyone knew what a Beehive round was and the damage it could cause.

The CO came running while shouting, "Stand down, stand down! You'll never get off this firebase alive!"

By that time, the other five gun pits had locked and loaded on them yelling, "You kill Sergeant Hall, and you'll all be dead!"

They knew the entire firebase had locked and loaded on them as they protected their own. They dropped their M16s, turned, and headed back to the helipad, shouting back, "We'll find you when this is over and kill you! Remember that!"

Everyone on the firebase shouted back, "And we'll find you and kill you!"

What came next took me by surprise. The CO informed me of my new assignment. Since I no longer had a gun section, I was assigned to deliver a prisoner to Tung Son Nuk. It was an American prisoner who could no longer take the war and shot himself in the foot. He had been placed under arrest for court martial. You didn't have to tell this guy that his intuition was right; the war was lost. My assignment was delivered to my hutch, informing me of all the details involving the transportation of this prisoner, which would take three days beginning the next morning on the first chopper. I was leaving the security of the firebase and now in route for a most unfavorable mission, which made me sick to my stomach.

Waiting near the helipad for the chopper, I felt alone and didn't even remember last night. My mind was concentrating on the details of this assignment. As far as weapons, I could only carry my personal .45 caliber pistol, an arm band with the initials MP, along with a set of handcuffs and key. I recalled this so-called prisoner shot himself in the foot, so I would say the advantage in safely delivering the prisoner was mine. At this point, my mind was too confused by recent events. At last, here came the chopper. The door gunner flipped off his harness, grabbed the mail bag, and headed for the Fire Direction Center. I climbed into the chopper, where the only other passenger onboard was my assignment. His foot was bandaged, and he had a crutch for support. We didn't need any introduction for he was already informed also on the details of his actions and the personnel involved in his transportation.

This person never said a word, which suited me just fine. In his mind, he had to address his actions and penalty according to the military code. At least in his mind, he was heading out of this hellhole alive and would have to live and deal with what he did.

I took off the shackles around his feet. "I know you can't run, and I also know I can catch you," I told him. I could tell by looking at him that his other problem was being hooked on China white. He wasn't going to be able to go home until he was clean, and that meant detox in the unknown. I said to him, "You're hooked on Scage, and I know it's going to be a while before you get back to the world."

I jumped off the chopper, ran into where our C rations were kept, and grabbed a bag of oranges and lemons with one bottle of Tabasco sauce. Returning, I gave them to him saying, "You better start sucking and drinking before we get there." The door gunner returned and, giving the thumbs-up to the chopper pilot, we were off to our first stop, Danang City, where we would continue on a C-130 transport to our destination south.

Again, my thoughts returned to the friendly fire accident and who it was. I was unsettled in my mind, and I had to deal with it just as my prisoner had to deal with his situation. Just then, the door gunner signaled to us that we were approaching our destination at Camp Eagle, just outside Da Nang City. This was where the C-130 would transport us to Tung Son Nuk, and I would then be released of my prisoner by the compound military police.

The speed in which I anticipated this assignment would conclude came to a crawl. I had completely ignored the injury and my prisoner's capability of dealing with the pain and adjusting to being handicapped. In this situation, and to Charlie, he was a sitting duck. The idea of being around these many people terrified me. And believe me, I could feel that the enemy was present. I was informed at headquarters that the sooner we got down to the airstrip, the sooner we could board and be on our way. The sooner, the better; I couldn't get there fast enough.

I never flew in anything but choppers while over here, so a C-130 was going to be a new experience and completely different. Instead of seats, we sat in netted slings with harnesses; and instead of windows, there were port holes. As we started to taxi down the runway, I was amazed how rough and loud this airship was. And as we picked up speed for lift off, I actually thought we were airborne until I looked out the port hole and noticed we were still on the runway still picking up speed. The vibrations and noise were deafening. I could only imagine what the landing was going to be like.

Once airborne, the motion seemed to put almost everyone to sleep, even my prisoner. One and a half hours later, we were landing, and just as I anticipated, the landing was one I'll never forget. We departed and started for the compound. Once outside the airport, I again sensed the presence of the enemy all around. The tension was extremely noticeable. I felt so much hate and anger coming from the South Vietnamese people that it reminded me of my first day in country and how even back then I sensed the same tension. For a moment I actually thought that maybe the friendly fire accident involved South Vietnamese families and I was thinking just maybe they knew it was me who did it. But that was impossible, and you could say I was a little jumpy and paranoid.

Once inside the compound, surrounded by barbed wire and twenty-four-hour guard watch, my feelings were still the same. It was unbelievable to see more Vietnamese inside the compound than outside. I could not understand how the commander in charge could allow this; barbershops, steam rooms and baths, massages and bars with entertainment, tailors, photographers, and women and children for anything and everything. How easy to overrun this camp. We reached our destination, and I thought my assignment was completed. However, the MPs would not take him from me as it was past 5:00 PM, and I would have to wait until tomorrow morning at 9:00 AM. They took us to a holding barracks, and they left for their entertainments. We had bunk beds.

"You take top," I told him. "If you jump, I'll hear you, plus you have nowhere to run, and I'll find you," I said.

I wanted to depart from this place right away and return to the firebase, but I was informed there were no more flights going north. I woke up senseless and had forgotten where I was. Then I realized I had a prisoner, so I jumped up and saw no one. I thought, just great, I lost my prisoner. What was I going to tell the MPs? Oh well, what are they going to do to me, send me home, back to the world, for losing a prisoner? Just then I saw a crutch come through the door. It was him, carrying a food tray.

"Here's breakfast!" he shouted.

"I had you long gone," I replied.

"I went for my piss test, and I'm clean," he said with delight. "The oranges, lemons, and Tabasco sauce worked," he said. "Now I can go back to the world and deal with what I did, shooting myself in the foot. I can deal with that. Thank you so much."

As I departed the compound, I was sensing my worst nightmare. Was this the end of South Vietnam? Had this country fallen? Did I volunteer to come here to be defeated? I just wanted to leave and return to my mountaintop. In the distance, I recognized from the chopper that naked little brown spot surrounded by miles of poison-green jungle. The anxiety of the morning was now erased from my mind, and the security of returning brought back my first memory of the fear I felt being put on top of a mountain. We were so far out and separated from the world and knew there was no possible way to receive any kind of support if overrun by Charlie.

As we circled the firebase, I saw my gun pit still in the situation I left it in. Then I caught sight of my gun crew. Evidently, they knew I was on that chopper, for they were drawing attention by waving like crazy, pounding their chests for only I knew what it meant. We were one, and as one, we would die together as one. I was proud of my men; they were the best. As the chopper landed, these guys were hurling sandbags and ammo boxes just to reach the landing pad.

"Chief, Chief!" shouted Fox. "We're a gun section again. It's about time you returned."

"I've got the gun crew back on schedule, Chief," remarked Gunner. "Welcome back."

"Chief," AG added, "we even have beer, black label. They flew it in when you left, you want one?"

"Back off, all of you. Let's go to the hutch!" Fox shouted.

"What did the investigation turn up?" I asked.

Fox continued, "CO said he'll get with you when you get back and that we could reform the gun section back as before."

"How many missions have you fired?" I asked.

"None," Fox cut in, "but you're back now so let's kick butt!"

"What's our ammo situation?" I asked.

Again Fox cut in, "We had so much ammo supplied to us that you'd think they're trying to tell us something."

"I'd better report to the CO, and I'll have that Black Label when I return," I said.

Halfway there, I ran into the CO.

"Chief," he said, "I was just on my way to your hutch. Let's head back to my hutch. Your gun section has been reformed and reactivated. It's unfortunate the accident happened."

"How many American soldiers were killed?" I asked.

"Ten," he continued. "But you wiped out the unit."

"If that eighth round hadn't jammed, I would have wiped out the whole squad," I remarked.

"It wasn't you fault, so let it go. We have reports of a big movement heading in our direction," he said, "let's concentrate on staying alive. Go get some rest."

As I started back to my hutch, my heart was breaking for the relatives of the men killed in the friendly fire. How will they take it knowing their loved ones were killed by a mistake, or will they even be told the truth? How could I let it go? Ten lives were lost. If I was still in the States doing burial detail with the Honor Guard and the question that kept going through my head at that time on how did these men lose their lives and to find out that their death was due to a mistake, then the whole Vietnam conflict was a mistake from start and my volunteering for this assignment to serve my country was now also a mistake. I could only justify their loss by making sure that I would also return in a box.

"Fire mission, fire mission! Battery adjust, battery adjust!" Fox came running toward me. "Chief, lets rock and roll!" he shouted.

For the next month, our fighting intensified greatly. Ammunition was being supplied more than regularly, and the amount also greatly increased. I was sensing the same fear and tension that came over me when I was in Tung Son Nuk; something wasn't right. I often wondered about our firebases farther up the Ashau Valley and if their fighting had also increased.

Fox dropped his headset and started yelling to us, "We just lost four firebases, and Charlie is on the move towards us!" As I put on my headset, I could hear the frantic voice of the FO (forward observer) directing the rounds as they hit. I could tell from his voice that this was the big movement headed toward us. Then there was nothing but static over the radio, and we lost communication. As night fell, so did our firing. Not one round was fired after we lost communication. There was not one fire mission or communication from that night forward, and I began to wonder if there were any firebases left.

I assigned guard duty among the gun section, and everyone seemed jumpy when listening sensors were posted 150 feet, rather than the regular fifty feet we usually posted them at. I informed the men that a movement was heading in our direction, and I wasn't taking any chances of being overrun. It wasn't until two in the morning that Gunner got me over to bunker fourteen.

"Put on the headset and listen," he said, as he pointed to sensor number 3.

Beep, beep, beep—beep, beep, beep—

"Could be monkeys," replied Gunner.

Beep, beep, beep—

Everyone's head automatically turned in the opposite direction, straining to see anything, for sensor number 1 was now beeping. If they were monkeys, it must be a herd, I thought. Good thing we moved the listening sensors further down the mountain. At least we would be able to spot whatever it was before it's too late. Just then, the listening sensor stopped beeping. All three went silent and stayed that way until red eye.

"Gunner," I called. "Let's get a detail and go down the mountain and pick up the listening sensors."

"Chief," he said, "we're not picking up the number three sensor on our headset." As I put on the headset I called out, "Throw a rock in number three's direction. Nothing. Now number two. Now number one. Let's get the detail together and go down the mountain and pick up one and two, and try to find three."

Well, number one and number two sensors were where we put them, but sure enough, number three was missing. We fanned out and did a search. I informed everyone that if we located sensor number three not to touch it because it could be booby-trapped. The number three sensor was located twenty-five feet further down the mountain. As I approached it I could tell that Charlie had been there. When Charlie realized we had posted listening sensors, they backed off taking sensor number three with them. I checked for any kind of booby-trap and found none. I went ahead and started to examine the sensor and to my surprise, not only did Charlie remove the listening sensor, he removed the battery inside the sensor and replaced it with a message to us on a piece of paper. All I could do was bust out laughing; everyone thought I had lost it right then and there.

I knelt there and realized that Charlie could not only write but also understood very well the English vocabulary. As I passed the message which was inside the sensor to the rest of the detail, one by one they also started laughing. We returned back up to the mountain top where the CO was waiting and watching intensely. Evidently some of the other guard bunkers had also heard movement last night. I handed him the piece of paper which was inside the sensor and watched and waited for his expression. After reading it, he just handed it over to his XO, who then passed it on to the others waiting. You could hear sneers, cursing, laughing, disbelief and astonishment for the message read: FUCK—U—GI—NUMBER 10—U—DIE—TONITE.

We had made contact with the enemy or should I say, the enemy had made contact with us. To me, watching the CO's expression seemed like he already knew that Charlie had surrounded us. Maybe there was more to the reports we received than he told us; for it sure seemed that Charlie also knew something that we didn't. Just then the XO asked all section chiefs to report to the CO's hutch ASAP.

You didn't have to tell me any more for I had put two and two together and I knew exactly what was happening and how these men were going to react to the news. I just hoped the CO knew he was going to start a possible mutiny or even a riot among the men and lose control of them. It all started to make sense now. Those four firebases that were overrun had no American units on them but has been replaced by the South Vietnamese Army without training which is the reason we were being supplied with so much ammo. I could only laugh to myself; angry me. I volunteered for Vietnam, remember, but as for the rest, they were volunteered by the rear commanding officer to sacrifice their lives so there was ample time for all necessary personnel stationed at Da Nang to escape the fall of the city; if that's what was really happening? As I listened to the reality of the situation, and the predicament we were in, the pride in serving my country was now being wiped out; just as a drop of water disturbs a perfect reflection.

We were the last ground combat unit remaining in the Ashau Valley. All other firebases were replaced by the South Vietnamese Army. And to make matters worse, we were going up against the biggest movement to overrun Da Nang City. Besides the four firebases already lost, we could expect the remaining nine to fall also since they had been replaced by the South Vietnamese Army too. The South Vietnamese Army did not have the training to operate a firebase or defend a mountain from such a large movement.

I recalled earlier in my tour, turning over Firebase 250 to the South Vietnamese Army. They brought their families and farm animals to live on top of the firebase and actually moved into our shitters for homes. We tried to explain that these were not for living in, but they would not listen and moved in children, farm animals, and all. You could eliminate any hope for any support by these firebases. We were on our own and the enemy had already made contact with us. And if was right, Charlie would save us for last knowing that all the other bases would be like taking candy from a baby.

How clever? Whoever ordered the replacements was only sending these people to their sure deaths and they didn't even know it. It was just enough to slow down the enemy front heading for Da Nang City. Oh, we were told that air support would be available to us along with regular ammo resupply and when the time came to evacuate the firebase air support would also be there.

I didn't tell my gun crew what was discussed in the meeting between the CO and section chiefs. I wasn't that stupid. I knew that my gun crew had their heads on straight, but to tell them that they had no choice but to stay on this firebase no matter what happened would take the fight out of them. It was going to be bad enough when they realized the truth about their fate and the endless efforts since they arrived in this country were for naught, along with all the other men before them who sacrificed their lives. And to be sacrificed now when it was obvious that this country was falling would not go over very well.

Six Chinook choppers appeared suddenly, each carrying ammo for our gun pits. Well, the rest of the day would be spent assembling the projectiles and storing them in the ammo bunkers. Our ammo supply had been doubled in stock just like the other gun pits so we had to keep our overstock in the crates they came in until room could be made once our fire missions were to be continued, which I knew wouldn't be long. You knew that Charlie was watching and if he had eyes he saw those choppers. It would be stupid to attack us when we just received resupply so they'll just attack and overrun one of the other nine firebases remaining in the Ashau Valley. One by one, they would destroy everything in their path knowing that our firebase will use up all our ammo giving support to the rest of the remaining nine who didn't know their fate was heading directly toward them. It would be an unstoppable massacre of men, women, children, and animals. This movement was an ugly, evil force that took no survivors and en route to conquer Saigon. I could only hope that Intelligence was preparing Saigon and also the remaining American units, if any, for a big show down. But, I couldn't concentrate on Saigon for if Da Nang City fell, it would be unstoppable to save Saigon.

"Fire mission, fire mission!"

"Battery adjust, battery adjust!"

Here we go. It's only a matter of time now. Charlie wouldn't waste time killing and destroying on his path to victory. I could only encourage my gun pit to operate at the best of its ability and kept reminding them how we would want them and how fast we would want them if we were in their situation. I didn't have to say any more as the intensity increased in every man to do anything and everything possible to save or try to save the lives of their friends in trouble. What our firebase didn't know was that when it came time for our turn to be overrun, there would be no support for us.

Suddenly Fox shouted, "They've lost it, they've lost it, it's over-run, damn gooks! Our firepower can't reach the remaining seven bases, cease-fire, cease-fire!" he screamed.

The XO once again informed all the section chiefs to join the CO in his hutch. New plan of attack I thought. If we couldn't help them, then the new plan of attack would be to save our ammo until the advancing front was within our range and surprise Charlie. Sure enough, just what 1 thought would happen, happened. As I left the CO's hutch and started back to my gun pit, we had no choice but to listen as one by one each firebase fell and there was nothing we could do for them. I could only hear and feel their terror.

In my mind were thoughts of how we were going to be evacuated. When the obvious was present, was the order for immediate evacuation or for the first sign of the enemy movement? Will it be the out of control situation when it's too late and every man for himself? Whatever it's going to be, it's still running and retreating in defeat.

You can't describe what it sounds like listening to the remaining bases fall, begging for support and for someone to do something. It's such a helpless feeling. Where was support for these bases? Were they not important enough to save? I hoped these men on this firebase were important enough in someone's eyes.

Suddenly, Fox shouted to me to get the headset. Big Brother had spotted the enemy movement coming within our range. I was surprised that Big Brother was even around, but I sure felt better knowing that at least now we have an eye in the sky, with night vision, which sure comes in handy against Charlie. Listening to Big Brother transmit back and forth with FDC, I realized Big Brother wasn't carrying any firepower. His main objective was to serve as our Forward Observer against the front since back in Da Nang all ammo was being sent to Saigon and the airstrip was being disassembled due to the retreat; all accept for the resupply of ammo for our base.

Fox turned to me with a troubled look, repeating what he just heard out loud, "What do they mean retreat, pull back to Saigon?"

All was interrupted by the sudden shouting coming from Big Brother. "Firebase, Fire—oh my god—Firebase, Firebase! FDC, FDC!" shouted Big Brother. "Put your CO on now!"

"Big Brother, Big Brother, this is the CO, over."

"Sir," came back Big Brother. "Big Brother is observing an enemy front that is heading in your direction and by the number of troops that I see, you better call for an immediate evacuation of your firebase now. I'll direct what rounds you have left to disperse and slow down Charlie, over."

"Affirmative, Big Brother," replied the CO. "If you could notify your air base for Chinook pickup?"

"Affirmative, firebase," replied Big Brother. "Now let's rock them with what you got left!" Little did Big Brother know that the conversation was not just between him and the CO. Fear was now visible in everyone; prayers, whimpers, silent cries of anger, and all eyes were filled with tears.

Well, we now lost this firebase. There's a joke commonly repeated in Vietnam about the actions of our leaders and it went like this—Do you know the difference between the Boy Scouts and the United States Military? The only difference between the Boy Scouts and the United States Military was that the Boy Scouts had adult leaders.

What now was on everybody's mind? We can't go North, or South, or East. Da Nang City is our only choice and it's being evacuated. Those Chinooks better get here soon; the ammo bunker was only half full.

"Fire mission, fire mission!"

Here we go. From this point forward, every move counts. For when this movement is over, we'll either be alive or dead. Even Da Nang City cannot help us as it will also fall, if it hasn't already. Where are those Chinooks?

Suddenly Big Brother came across the radio. There was excitement in his voice, "Firebase, firebase! Keep pumping out those rounds. You got a direct hit. Man, I see bodies going everywhere, yes, yes! You've got them pinned. Keep it coming keep it coming, oh baby! What's happening, firebase, keep it coming?"

"Big Brother, Big Brother," came back the reply from FDC, "We have extinguished our ammo, contact air base Da Nang City for pickup!"

"Affirmative," replied Big Brother, "but you should know you stirred up an ant nest and their double timing it to you guys. Returning to Da Nang, good luck, over and out."

Good luck? There's no good luck involved, I thought. If those choppers were not here in thirty minutes. there would be nothing to come out for. That's reality! The perimeter was secured by all able bodies. Gun Pit One had already made contact with Charlie, and the fire fight had begun. Where were those choppers? The procedure now was to secure for a gun pit overrun. Good thing I personally booby-trapped my gun pit. I'll be damned if Charlie was going to take over my gun pit; I hid some surprises set on timers just for them.

The men were informed to withdraw to the helipad as soon as the choppers landed. I also informed them that I would weld the breech of the gun by using a Willie Peter grenade at the last second. I still had two Beehive rounds left, and those were used especially on an overrun. The Beehive rounds would explode right out of the tube, sending millions of steel arrows in every direction and stripping a person or animal clean down to the bones. It only took one man to set everything off, so if this was to be my last mission; I wasn't going to screw it up. I volunteered for Vietnam, so it was only right that I carry out the final chapter.

As the sounds of the claymores were being set off by each gun pit, the thought of the choppers was completely forgotten. The only thoughts present were those of anger and also of what type of death I would experience since all I was seeing was either being shot or stabbed. It took three or four against one, and it made me feel good though that it took that many to take us down.

"Choppers, choppers!" someone yelled.

I looked at my gun section, each crying and trying to hold it back. Nobody wanted to die. "Go, go, go!" I yelled. "I'll cover, got to set off my surprises!"

As the last timer was set inside the excess gunpowder bunker, the sounds of mortars exploding on top was a clear signal to get out now, but I hadn't welded the breech shut to destroy the gun, and I had to do this as I cleared the last step out of the bunker. Tracers from an M-60 cut right beside my left arm throwing me back against the opening of the bunker. I just knew I'd been shot, but I wasn't. One of the choppers was giving support to the right side of my gun pit where Charlie started to break through.

I guess the door gunner wasn't expecting someone to charge out of a bunker, and I wasn't expecting a chopper to nearly land on me as I busted through the opening of the bunker after seeing my chance. Once the door gunner saw that I was American, I charged for the gun to weld it shut. I didn't have time to fire the Beehives and as long as the chopper was giving support, I could set a timer to explode the gun and the Beehive rounds together. No sooner was I done, the chopper took off with a one twenty-two rocket just barely missing it.

Looking to the top of the firebase, where the helipad was, you could see the last stand by the amount of small arms fire being dispersed. Two choppers were left and if I didn't get on one of those, you could kiss my butt goodbye. I had no intention of doing that. What did surprise me was how many rockets missed us.

As we rose above the firebase, I spotted my gun pit for the last time. My booby traps were going off just as planned, sending balls of fire in every direction. I realized just then that I had lost all my personal property which I had collected during my tour in Vietnam. I had nothing left. All the letters from my pen pals, my friends, my sister, my money, even my "Dear John" letter were gone. My life seemed to flash right before me as the explosions continued, and we headed away.

Da Nang Airport was under attack as we landed. People were running in every direction trying to take cover. My gun section was now lost in a sea of people. The South Vietnamese Army was informing the commanding officer that a C-130 transport was on its way to evacuate us and that all firearms should be turned over to them so they could protect the airstrip, which was under siege. We could keep our flak jackets. It was hard to believe but here we were in the middle of a fire fight with no weapons and only our flak jackets to protect us.

We were filed underground, six to eight feet, shoulder to shoulder, then closed in by a trapdoor while the enemy was making their way down to where we were. The ground shook from the incoming and the thought of the North Vietnamese Army finding us there, trapped underground, was too much to handle. I just hoped that they didn't park anything on top of the trapdoor. No sooner had I that thought than a mad rush pushed everyone out gasping for air, like a flash flood.

Outside was no better. No plane in sight and no South Vietnamese Army to protect us. It only figured there never was a

C-130 transport and our weapons were taken away so they could protect themselves and not us. I guess I couldn't blame them for lying to us, as many times I'm sure, the United Stated lied to them.

Suddenly a roar screamed through the darkness. You didn't have to tell anyone what it was. Everyone was making a mad dash for the C-130 transport even before it landed. Once again, we had cheated death by the skin of our teeth but not so for all the brave defenders of this county. I thought of those left behind to fend for themselves. I'll never forget them!

You would think this would be the end of my war, but I did not forget about the threat to my life. Shall I repeat it? It never left my mind. For forty-six years, I've been watching my back and hearing the words *When this is over, we'll find you and you'll wish you were never born. You're a dead man. You killed our buddies!* The curse had followed me back to the world. The war was over, but my personal war just continued. I was disconnected from the world, trusting no one. For every pit fall, I had my guilt and shame, which I accepted as deserving of them for all the lives lost in the war.

Looking back I wonder what my life path would have been had I not entered this country. Is there really a reason for why all things happen? As I sit watching my wife of thirty-six years sleeping, I recognize how much she has endured; three broken ribs, brain surgery for a baseball-sized tumor, a broken hip, and now she's lost in thought not knowing where she's at. That's the hard part. I've watched this woman in so much emotional and physical pain beginning in childhood to the present date.

There's really no answer as to where tumors come from. I've read that we all are born with some type of tumor, which lies dormant until some traumatic event happens in life, which activates the tumor to grow. I asked questions from the doctors as to how long it took to get that size, but there was no answer. It could have been growing for thirty years. And then there was the medication to make my wife able to withstand the pain from the surgery and post-surgery, which did not work. The medical field failed completely when they didn't take into consideration the side effects from the combination of mental medications there were pumping her with. They could not understand why she was so confused and combative. Couldn't they understand that the brain could not respond to the medications because it had just been traumatized from being cut wide open and it would be as I was told up to a year, if lucky, for the brain to heal.

My wife is part of a percentage of violated people, both physically and mentally, whose life was destroyed before it was ever started. Now I knew the traumatic experience she went through as a baby and later being disowned by her family. I knew for a fact because I raised her two mixed baby girls. At that time they were one, Vi, and five years old. Today she doesn't recognize me or them.

Is there a reason for our existence, our purpose? Is there a reason why things happen in our lives? When each of us was born, was it that someday our paths would cross? I was born on a dirt floor in a third-world country. My mother was the only means of my survival. She was a thief, beggar, prostitute—whatever it took to feed us. My wife was born in a hospital, lived in a house, and was the daughter of a strawberry farmer who could very well support his family.

There's not a day that goes by that I don't apologize to my mother for not making more of myself for all the sacrifices she made. Even to this date, I don't know how old she was or when she passed. Was the reason things happened in order for me to come to this country rather than stay where I was born? Certain events had to occur.

Did the horrific events that my wife endured as a little innocent girl, which changed her life and destroyed her brain, had to occur for certain events to happen? But then there's one thing we all know: it was out of our control.

As I sit and watch over her as she tries to sleep, I know at any moment she could sit up screaming, wanting to get out of bed. I would restrain her from doing it. After her breaking her upper femur, she can't walk on her own, but she doesn't understand, which only increases the screaming and confusion. This is a daily pattern, but different times of the day when they occur.

In the dark, I would sit and think of the war and how I saw grown men cry for lack of sleep in our underground bunker where rats, snakes, spiders, roaches and centipedes crawled in the dark. I myself fell asleep on a cot, and when I got up, the imprint of my body was made by baby pink rates. The mama rat used my body heat to have her babies. I was informed to shake my cot on the side of the mountain like everyone else. No big thing.

I heard the neurosurgeon remark, "This is a slow-growing tumor, possibly thirty years to get to that size. As soon as we can stabilize your wife, we can do radiation so the remaining tumor wrapped around the blood vessels in her brain will shrink."

In my mind I could hear those words. No big thing.

Looking into her eyes, I could see her confusion. Not being able to put words together to express herself, but that's how she came out of surgery, and after she broke her upper right femur, she couldn't walk. Seeing the amount of medication she was issued and the return visits to the hospital due to the side effects completely turned her world upside down. From one nursing home to another, I followed, staying by her side and assuring her everything will be all right. We just needed to stabilize her for radiation to address the remaining tumor.

After eleven months, a seizure put her back into the hospital, where I was told the tumor had grown back twice the size. It was thirty-seven beautiful years. Coming back from the Vietnam War as a loose cannon, she grounded me and saved my life! Having three daughters, nine grandchildren, and two great-grandchildren with approximately two hundred animals that she rescued to me is the greatest story ever told. Love you, darling, forever!

grunts in the field or the tactical operations center personnel," he says. "The gun battery crew
entered the coordinates provided to them cor-
rectly and was not at fault."

In early August, Lt. Col. Rocco Negris stood
before the specially handpicked men of D Co.,
3rd Bn., 21st Inf. "No taking chances. No hero-
ics," he told them. "This is our last patrol." For
three days, Aug. 8-10, the grunts beat the bush in
the DaNang "rocket belt." Several were wounded
by booby traps. Spec. 4 James McVicar stepped
on a half-buried c-ration can, which exploded,
spraying him with shrapnel. Evacuated to the
95th Evacuation Hospital in DaNang, he was the
last line infantryman wounded in the war.

Six men of Fire Team Bravo, 2nd Squad, 3rd
Platoon, D Company, led by Lt. John Vermilion,
were the last to be Lifted out of the field by helicopter on that history-making mission. When
the entire operation was completely done, Sgt.
Al Alcala exclaimed: "God, I can't believe we're
finally going home—that it's over!" CBS reporter
Phil Jones accompanied that final patrol. "For the
grunts," he proclaimed, "the Vietnam War is over."

But it had been hard slogging to get to that
juncture of history. Roger Drouet was among
those extracted from the field on Aug. 10. An
M-60 machine gunner, he participated in 25
aerial missions from January through July. "We
stayed in the jungle two weeks at a time," he
recalled, "sometimes inserted by helicopter into
hot Lzs. We set up listening posts on trails outside night defensive positions, which were often
probed by sappers. Memories of the sounds,
sights and smells of these operations never go
away."

Rich Wengatz arrived in Vietnam on Jan. 1,1972. An 11D20—armor recon specialist—he started out with the 2nd Sqdn., 11th ACR at Pho Loi. On May 28, he went to the 2nd Bn., 1st Inf., and finally C Co., 2nd Bn., 21st Inf., from June 15 to Aug.12. His path to Vietnam was unique. "I was a Department of the Army volunteer who selected the option for Vietnam," he said. "On the last night my unit was in the field, my squad drew the short straw and set up along a known NVA trail with an OP and tripwires/Claymores."

Also arriving in January, Rich Waldrop ended up in the mortar platoon of HHC in battalion headquarters at the base of Hill 321. He clearly remembers the last stand down: "As I stood in the final formation where we furled the colors, I realized I was part of a historical moment in the Vietnam War and was proud to have served."

Gun bunnies of B Btry., 3rd Bn., 82nd Field Artillery were part of that history, too. Ron Fox vividly recalls the final mission: "The battery stayed out for another day to cover the infantry as they pulled out of the field. There was a massive fire for effect, all six guns firing 20 to 30 rounds each and then Gun #4 fired one final round. The U.S. flag that flew over the firebase was taken down and so ended the U.S. artillery's role in Vietnam."

George Whitehouse was the section chief of the Fire Direction Center. "That final, ceremonial round went off of Hill 260 at 1100 hours on Aug. 10," he says.

"I remember thinking this is really it for me [he had been with three other artillery units that stood.

About the Author

Michael Hall's life was put on a path in life in which it traveled in many directions, with crossroads, some filled with happiness and sadness, which is part of life. So always remember, a good day starts by waking up sucking air!

CPSIA information can be obtained
at www.ICGtesting.com
Printed in the USA
LVHW021438230322
714164LV00006BA/1355